Letts
gets *you* through

KS2 GRAMMAR, PUNCTUATION & SPELLING
SATs SUCCESS
REVISION GUIDE

Ages 7–11

KS2
GRAMMAR,
PUNCTUATION
& SPELLING
SATs
REVISION
GUIDE

SHELLEY WELSH

Contents

Grammar Terms

Creating Sentences

Sentence Features

Punctuation

Vocabulary and Spelling

SATs Practice Questions

Grammar Terms

Types of nouns

Common nouns are naming words for people, places, animals and things. They also name things or ideas that cannot be seen or touched.

Proper nouns are the actual names of people, places, days of the week, months of the year, planets, titles of books, films, plays… it's a long list! They always begin with a capital letter.

Common nouns

Here are some common nouns:

| a **boy** | a **dog** | **pens** | the **football** | the **table** |

Some nouns, called collective nouns, name a group of things or people.

| the football **team** | the Year 6 **class** |
| a **murder** of crows | a **herd** of cows |

Other nouns are names of feelings or ideas, things you cannot see or touch.

| anger | temptation | courage | love |

Proper nouns

Proper nouns **always** begin with a capital letter.

| James | Thursday | Jupiter | The Hobbit | Germany |

Top tip!

You might find it easier to remember that names of places and people are **proper nouns** if you remember that **p**lace, **p**eople and **p**roper all start with **p**!

Keywords

Nouns ➤ Naming words for people, places, animals and things

Common nouns ➤ Nouns for people, animals, objects, feelings or ideas

Proper nouns ➤ Nouns that name particular things. They begin with a capital letter

Noun phrases

A phrase is a group of words that work together as if they are one word.

A **noun phrase** is a phrase that acts like a noun. The main word is a noun.

the football	the clock	an apple	a tree

She kicked **her football** as hard as she could.

Her football is the noun phrase – the noun **football** is linked to **her**.

Adding more information to a noun turns it into an **expanded noun phrase**.

expanded noun phrase

The beautiful blue butterfly landed on **the pretty pink flower**.

noun   noun

Both **the beautiful blue butterfly** and **the pretty pink flower** are expanded noun phrases.

Keywords

Noun phrase ➤ A phrase where a noun is the main word

Expanded noun phrase ➤ A phrase with a noun as its main word with other words that tell us more about that noun

Have a go! Look around your home and make a list of five nouns you can see. Turn them first of all into noun phrases, then into expanded noun phrases.

Test yourself

❶ Write one example of a common noun, a proper noun and a noun that cannot be seen or touched.

❷ Identify and name the different types of nouns you can find in these sentences:

a. When the astronauts landed on Mars, they took photographs of the Earth.

b. Ben displayed great courage when he saw the bees coming towards him.

Present and past tense

A **verb** is a word that can tell you about an action, such as run, skate, sing. A verb can also tell you about a state of being, such as **to be**, **to love**, **to enjoy**, **to have**.

Every sentence **must** contain a verb.

> I **watch** television every evening.

(The verb **to watch** is in the **simple present tense**. The present tense is used when we are talking about an event or state of being that is happening **now**.)

> The dog **was** absolutely wild.

(The verb **to be** is in the **simple past tense**. The past tense is used when we are talking about an event or state of being that has already happened.)

> I **showed** my friend my new shoes.

(The verb **to show** is in the **past** tense.)

Present and past progressive tense

We can show that an action is/was continuous by using the progressive tenses.

> I **am watching** television.

(present progressive)

> I **was watching** television.

(past progressive)

Present and past perfect tense

We can show that an action is/was completed by using the perfect tenses.

The **present perfect** tense is formed from the present tense of the verb **have** and the past participle of the main verb. The **past perfect** tense is formed from the past tense of the verb **have** and the past participle of the main verb.

> She **has played** outside all day so now she is tired.

(present tense of **have**; past participle of **play**)

> Mum **had brought** the washing in before the rain started.

(past tense of **have**; past participle of **bring**)

Keywords

Verb ➤ A word for an action or state of being

Present ➤ A verb tense showing what is happening now

Past ➤ A verb tense showing what has happened

Present progressive ➤ A verb tense showing a continuous action in the present

Past progressive ➤ A verb tense showing a continuous action in the past

Present perfect ➤ A verb tense formed from the present tense of the verb 'have' + past participle of the main verb

Past perfect ➤ A verb tense formed from the past tense of the verb 'have' + past participle of the main verb

Top tip! To find the verb, first find the person, animal or thing in the sentence and see what they are **doing** or **being**.

Have a go!

Write a diary entry about what you did at the weekend.

Test yourself

❶ Circle the most appropriate verb forms in these sentences:

a. I drank/was drinking my juice when the phone rang.

b. Suddenly, the car crashed/was crashing into the brick wall.

c. I eat/am eating my tea every evening before I watch/am watching television.

d. While we had/were having a picnic, it started to rain.

e. Joe was jumping/is jumping on his trampoline when it began to rain.

Modal verbs

Modal verbs are verbs that change the meanings of other verbs.

As well as showing tenses, these verbs show where something is **certain**, **probable**, **possible** – or not.

Example sentence	Uncertain	Possible	Probable	Certain
I **may** be going swimming this evening. I **would** offer to take you with me but there **might** not be enough room in the car as we **could** be taking our neighbours.	✓			
There **can** be as many as fifty children in the swimming pool at any given time.		✓		
Sam and Tom haven't eaten very much all day so they **must** be hungry by now.			✓	
The other team **will** be hard to beat so I **must** try hard to score a goal.				✓

Here are some modal verbs:

can	could	may	might		shall	should
will	would	must	ought to			

Listen up 3

Keywords

Modal verbs ➤ Verbs that show possibility or likelihood

Adverb ➤ A word that tells us more about a verb or an adjective

Adverbs of possibility

Sometimes we use **adverbs** to show how likely something is.

Here are some examples:

perhaps	likely	surely	certainly	definitely
maybe	possibly	clearly	obviously	probably

> Joseph had **clearly** finished his breakfast because there wasn't a scrap left on his plate.

The adverb **clearly** shows us that it is **certain** that Joseph has finished.

> The dog walker **probably** hadn't seen the "Please keep off the Grass!" sign.

The adverb **probably** shows us that it is **quite likely** the dog walker hadn't seen the sign.

> Taking exercise is **definitely** good for our health.

The adverb **definitely** shows us that the writer believes **without any doubt** that exercise is good for our health.

 Modal verbs are followed by a verb in its basic form.

(modal verb) (basic verb form)

I **might finish** my homework on time this week.

Top tip!

 **Have a go!**

Write the adverbs of possibility in the table above on a timeline, from least possible to most likely.

 **Test yourself**

❶ **Underline one adverb in each sentence that indicates a degree of possibility (from certainty to uncertainty).**

a. I am definitely unable to go swimming tonight.

b. He'll likely come tomorrow.

c. Perhaps if you tried harder you would succeed.

d. You should probably leave early tomorrow because it is going to snow.

Adjectives

Adjectives are words that give us more information about the noun in a sentence.

> Stanley was a cat.

> Stanley was a **black** and **white** cat with a **chubby** face and **pointy** ears.

Black and **white** describe the colour of Stanley, **chubby** describes his face and **pointy** describes his ears.

Adjectives make sentences more interesting and can be used to create imaginative and exciting descriptions.

Use a thesaurus to find exciting adjectives. Remember, a thesaurus gives you **synonyms**, which are words that have the same or nearly the same meaning as another word.

Adjectives that compare two nouns

Adjectives that compare two nouns usually end in **er**, but look what happens when the adjective has more than two syllables:

Adjective: **tall**:

> Sam is **taller** than Aisha.

Adjective: **beautiful**:

> Cinderella is **more beautiful** than her step-sisters.

Keywords

Adjective ➤ A word that describes a noun

Synonym ➤ A word that means the same or almost the same as another word

Adjectives that compare more than one noun

Adjectives that compare more than one noun in a sentence usually end in **est**, but look what happens when the adjective ends in **y** or has more than two syllables:

Adjective: **short**:   Aisha is the **shortest** of all the children.

Adjective: **pretty**:   Orla has the **prettiest** outfit of all the girls on the stage.

Adjective: **impressive**:   Dan's hat is the **most impressive** in all the school.

Before writing a description, list some useful adjectives. For example, when writing about reaching a mountain summit, you might use words like:

agonising cold
frost-bitten fingers
snow-capped peaks
breath-taking view

Have a go! Use a thesaurus to find as many synonyms for 'nice' and 'bad' as you can. Remember, synonyms are words that have the same or nearly the same meaning as another word. We will be looking at these on pages 60 and 61.

Test yourself

❶ Underline the adjectives in the sentence below:

Once the electric fence had been activated, even the most desperate animals couldn't escape.

❷ Now write two sentences of your own using interesting adjectives.

❸ Write two sentences that each compare the noun <u>cat</u>, using the following adjectives:

a. naughty

b. sensible.

A **conjunction** links two words, phrases or clauses together.

Conjunctions that link two words or phrases

Some conjunctions link two words, phrases or clauses together as an equal pair or are equal in importance. These are called **coordinating conjunctions**.

and	but	or	nor	yet	so	for

In this sentence, apples and oranges link together as an equal pair:

> Maeve likes apples **and** oranges.

In these sentences, the two clauses are linked together in equal importance:

> Stanley is clever **but** finds science challenging.

Keywords

Conjunction ➤ Links two words, phrases or clauses

Coordinating conjunction ➤ Links two words, phrases or clauses of equal importance

Subordinate clause ➤ A clause which depends on the main clause to make sense

Main clause ➤ A clause that can make sense as a sentence

Subordinating conjunction ➤ Joins a subordinate clause to a main clause

Listen up 5

Conjunctions that join a subordinate clause to a main clause

Some conjunctions join a **subordinate clause** to a **main clause**.

A subordinate clause starts with a **subordinating conjunction** and **does not** make sense on its own. A main clause **does** make sense on its own.

Here are some common conjunctions that join subordinate clauses to main clauses:

after   although   as   because   before   if   once   since   than

that   though   unless   until   when   whenever   where   whether   while

> main clause   subordinate clause
>
> Dev played football **until** it started raining.
>
> subordinating conjunction

The subordinate clause can come before the main clause:

> subordinate clause   main clause
>
> **Although** it was sunny, the children kept their coats on.
>
> subordinating conjunction

Top tip! To identify the subordinate clause, find the subordinating conjunction in a sentence then read it, followed by the clause that comes after it. Ask yourself, does it make sense on its own?

 **Have a go!** Choose a page from the book you are reading and copy some sentences containing subordinate clauses. Highlight the main clause in one colour and the subordinate clause in another.

 **Test yourself**

❶ What is the difference between a main clause and a subordinate clause?

❷ How many subordinating conjunctions can you think of?

❸ Write two sentences, one containing the coordinating conjunction <u>but</u> and one containing the subordinating conjunction <u>unless</u>.

Pronouns

A **pronoun** can be used instead of a noun. Look at these sentences:

| proper noun | noun | noun | noun |

Stella visited a **castle** with her **mum** and **dad**.

Her **mum** and **dad** said the **castle** was ancient.

| noun | noun | noun |

We can replace some of the nouns with pronouns:

Stella visited a **castle** with her **mum** and **dad**. **They** said **it** was ancient.

| pronoun for mum and dad | pronoun for castle |

The following are personal pronouns:

| I | you | he | she | it | we |
| me | him | her | us | them | they |

The **children** gave the books to **Stella**. ⟶ **They** gave the books to **her**.

Relative pronouns

A **relative pronoun** introduces a **relative clause** that says more about a noun.

The following are relative pronouns:

that **which** **who** **whose** **where** **when**

relative clause

My best **friend**, **who** lives by the sea, is moving to London.

noun   relative pronoun

relative clause

The **children**, **whose** parents were held up, stayed behind in the library.

noun   relative pronoun

Possessive pronouns

A **possessive pronoun** shows ownership.

That book is **mine**. The one on the shelf is **hers**.

my book   her book

The following are possessive pronouns:

> mine
> yours
> his/hers/its
> ours
> theirs

Listen up 6

Keywords

Pronoun ➤ A word that replaces a noun

Relative pronoun ➤ The words 'who', 'which', 'that', 'whose', 'when' and 'where', that introduce a relative clause

Relative clause ➤ A subordinate clause introduced by a relative pronoun

Possessive pronoun ➤ A word to show ownership

Parent tip! Encourage your child to use relative pronouns to create longer sentences.

Have a go! Write the headings relative and possessive pronouns. Jot down examples of each kind that you find when reading a chapter of your book. Can you write one sentence containing each type of pronoun?

Test yourself

❶ What nouns do the pronouns <u>it</u> and <u>them</u> refer to in this sentence?

Fred and Aisha stared into the gloomy distance. <u>It</u> seemed to pulsate with danger and filled <u>them</u> with fear.

❷ Rewrite both these sentences so that they each contain a possessive pronoun:

That bike isn't your bike! That bike is my bike!

❸ Insert a suitable relative pronoun into this sentence:

The boys' books, ... were scattered all over the floor, had been expensive birthday presents.

Adverbs

Adverbs can give us more information about the verb. They **describe** the verb. Many adverbs that say **how** or **when** an action is carried out end in the suffix **ly** or **ally**.

quick**ly**   hard   magic**ally**   well
frantic**ally**   ridiculous**ly**

Benji **ate** his dinner **slowly**.
verb   adverb

adverb   verb   verb   adverb
Sam **suddenly collapsed** with exhaustion. He had **tried hard** to win but without success.

Adverbials

An **adverbial** is a word, phrase or clause that gives us more information about a verb (how, where, when, how often) or clause.

- slowly, quickly, crossly – **how**
- here, somewhere, far away – **where**
- soon, now, still, yesterday – **when**
- often, usually, occasionally – **how often**

where   when
Far, far away, a dragon **still** roams the hills, **occasionally** breathing fire **angrily** on the people below.
how often   how

Hannah stared **into the far distance** to find the tiny boat bobbing on the waves.
an adverbial saying where

We will be leaving for Paris **in one week**. ← an adverbial saying when

Adverbs saying more about adjectives

Adverbs can also say more about an adjective in the sentence.

I've burned the cake – it is **completely ruined**.

adverb adjective

Ushma was **quite excited** as she opened her presents.

Fronted adverbials

To create a different effect, put the adverb or adverbial at the front, or start, of the sentence, followed by a comma. This is called a **fronted adverbial**.

Cautiously, Tom crept into the gloomy darkness of the gaping cave.

The adverb **cautiously** at the start, or front, of the sentence helps to build tension.

Keywords

Adverb ➤ A word that tells us more about a verb (how, where, when), an adjective, another adverb or a whole clause

Adverbial ➤ A word, phrase or clause that gives us more information about a verb (how, where, when, how often) or clause

Fronted adverbial ➤ An adverb or adverbial at the start of a sentence

To help you find an adverb that describes **how**, find the verb in the sentence first.

Top tip!

Have a go!

Listen to a documentary or news programme and make a note of as many adverbs and adverbials as you can hear.

Test yourself

Listen up

7

① Underline any adverbs or adverbials in these sentences:

a. Desperately, Erin wriggled through the gap and in a matter of minutes was free.

b. In the middle of the night, the wind suddenly died down and soon the children were fast asleep.

② Write a sentence with an adverb that describes where something happens.

③ Write a sentence containing an adverb which tells us more about an adjective.

Listen up
8

Prepositions

Prepositions usually come before a noun or pronoun. They show the relationship between the noun or pronoun and other words in the clause or sentence. They often describe position or time.

Prepositions showing position

Some prepositions show position.

> Bert slid **behind** the sofa when the monster appeared **on** television.

Behind shows where Bert was in relation to the sofa and **on** shows where the monster was in relation to the television.

> The dog was sleeping **under** the bed.

Under shows where the dog was sleeping in relation to the bed.

Keyword

Preposition ➤ A word that shows the relationship between the noun or pronoun and other words in the clause or sentence

Top tip!

Words such as **before** and **since** can act as either prepositions or as conjunctions.
- I haven't seen Gran since Christmas. (preposition)
- Ben went to bed early since he'd been up all night. (conjunction)

NOUN
ADJECTIVE
ADVERB
LEARN ENGLISH
CONJUNCTION
PREPOSITION
VERB
PRONOUN

Prepositions indicating time

Some prepositions show time.

> I haven't eaten **since** my breakfast this morning.

Since tells us how long it has been since the person last ate.

> Every day, the teacher rings the bell **at** 9.00 am.

At tells us when the teacher rings the bell.

> **In** the evenings, I like a cup of hot chocolate and a biscuit.

The phrase 'In the evenings' (the preposition being **in**) tells us when the person likes a cup of hot chocolate and a biscuit.

Common prepositions

These are common prepositions.

about	after	behind	in	of	since	under
above	at	by	into	off	through	up
across	before	during	near	on	to	with

Create a set of instructions on how to get from the front door of your house into your bedroom. How many prepositions have you used?

① Underline the prepositions in the following sentences:

I went to my room and in it was the biggest mess imaginable! After I had cleared it, I went to the kitchen and sat at the table. Later, Mum called me to help in the garden. What a day!

Determiners

A **determiner** is a word that comes before a noun to tell us whether the noun is specific (known) or general (unknown).

The determiners the, a and an

- **the** is used when the noun is specified as known.
- **a** and **an** are used when the noun is specified as unknown.

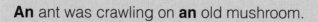

The cat ran off and ended up on **a** ship heading to **the** island.

| **the** is used because it refers to a specific cat (known) | **a** is used because it was just any ship (unknown) | **the** is used because it refers to a specific island (known) |

Remember to use **an** before words beginning with a vowel.

An ant was crawling on **an** old mushroom.

Other determiners

This, **that**, **these** and **those** can also be determiners.

This fishing rod doesn't belong to **these** boys.

That girl caught all **these** fish!

Some, **every**, **all**, **none** and **lots of** act as determiners. They show amounts.

Some children eat **lots of** fruit. **Every** person in my family eats **a lot of** vegetables.

Possessive determiners

Possessives such as **my**, **your**, **his**, **her**, **its**, **our** and **their** can also act as determiners. They show ownership of the noun that immediately follows.

My old aunt was invited to tea at **their** house.

'my' tells us whose aunt it is

'their' tells us whose house it is

Maya told me that **her** dog had eaten **its** collar so she couldn't walk to **my** house.

Top tip! Never use an apostrophe in the possessive determiner **its**. **It's always** means **it is**.

Parent tip! It's easy for children to forget to use **an** before words starting with a vowel. Look around the house together and use **an** before objects beginning with vowels.

Keywords

Determiner ➤ A word that introduces a noun such as 'the', 'a', 'some' and 'those'

Possessive determiner ➤ Shows ownership of the noun that immediately follows

Have a go! Write a paragraph that contains five of the following determiners: a, an, the, some, those, these, this, that.

Test yourself

① Underline the determiners in the following sentences:

Some children were heading towards the beach when an adult came towards them waving a flag. It was the coastguard. He told them the weather had changed and they couldn't go in the sea. The children turned back up the path.

② Write an instruction for when to use the determiner <u>an</u>.

Grammar Terms

This mind map will help you remember all the main points from this topic. Have a go at drawing your own mind map.

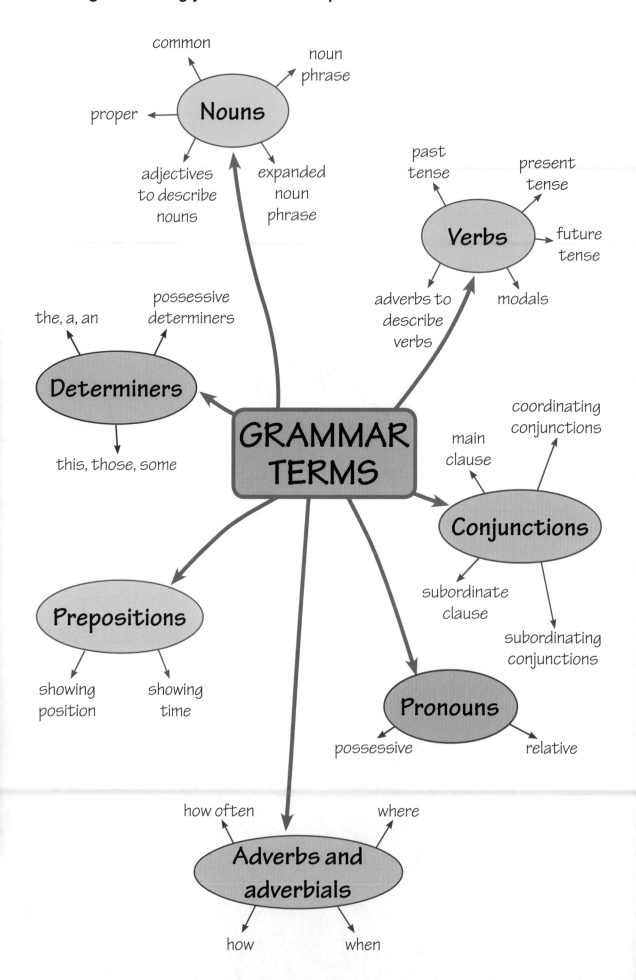

1 Write the nouns in the box below in the correct columns of the table. **(3 marks)**

fear	hand	dog	strength	Antarctica
despair	flock	flower	July	house
pity	Prince George	Jupiter	United Kingdom	bravery

Proper nouns	Common nouns	
	Nouns we can see or touch	**Nouns we can't see or touch**

2 Write this present tense sentence in the simple past tense.　　**(1 mark)**

　 I eat my dinner quickly.

....

3 Underline the modal verbs in these sentences.　　**(3 marks)**

　 a. My mother couldn't finish the horror story.

　 b. The heating has been on so you must be warm now.

　 c. Would it be possible to leave the theatre now?

4 Write a sentence which contains a main clause and a subordinate clause.　　**(1 mark)**

....

5 Underline the coordinating conjunctions in this short passage.　　**(2 marks)**

　 We had salad and bread for tea but nothing at bedtime. The next morning we were tired and hungry. There was some cereal on the table yet no sign of any milk.

6 Underline the five pronouns in the sentence below.　　**(2 marks)**

　 My sister hurt her finger at the park and she had to have it bandaged. The nurse praised her for being brave and she gave her a special plaster.

7 Underline the adverbs in the following sentence.　　**(2 marks)**

　 Harry tiptoed carefully down the creaky steps. He soon reached the cellar where he stumbled awkwardly over a carelessly discarded pizza box.

Phrases

A **phrase** is a group of words that acts in the same way as one word: it might contain a **verb**, a **noun**, an **adjective**, an **adverb**, a **preposition** or a **conjunction**. A phrase doesn't make sense on its own as a sentence.

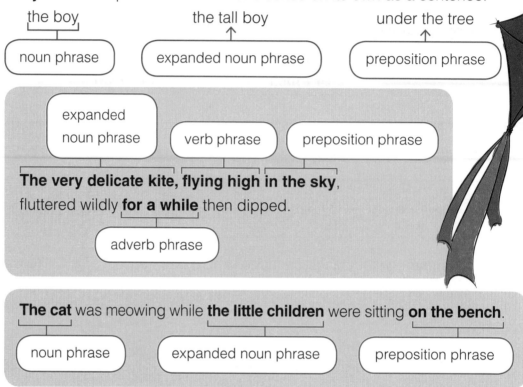

the boy
noun phrase

the tall boy
expanded noun phrase

under the tree
preposition phrase

expanded noun phrase

verb phrase

preposition phrase

The very delicate kite, flying high in the sky, fluttered wildly **for a while** then dipped.

adverb phrase

The cat was meowing while **the little children** were sitting **on the bench**.

noun phrase

expanded noun phrase

preposition phrase

Clauses

A **clause** contains a verb and can make sense as a sentence. A clause can be a **main clause** or a **subordinate clause**. Subordinate clauses are introduced by a subordinating conjunction. (These are covered on pages 12 and 13.)

- This sentence is a short clause with one noun phrase and one verb:

  The kettle boiled.

- This sentence is a longer clause:

  I was wearing my wellies in the park.

- This sentence has two clauses of equal importance. The clauses are joined by the coordinating conjunction **but**.

  main clause   main clause

  It was raining **but** we didn't care.

Clauses (continued)

- This sentence has a main clause followed by a subordinate clause:

main clause	subordinate clause
We put our coats on	because it was raining.

'We put our coats on' is the main clause because it makes sense alone; 'because it was raining' is a subordinate clause – it only makes sense **with** the main clause.

- This sentence has a subordinate clause followed by a comma, followed by a main clause:

subordinate clause	main clause
Although it was raining,	Sasha and his friends had a picnic.

'Sasha and his friends had a picnic' is the main clause because it makes sense alone. 'Although it was raining,' is a subordinate clause – it only makes sense with the main clause. If you start your sentence with the subordinate clause, you need to follow it with a comma.

Keywords

Phrase ➤ A group of words that work together as if they are one word

Clause ➤ Contains a verb and can act as a sentence. It can be a main clause or subordinate clause

 **Look for interesting noun phrases or expanded noun phrases in any book you are reading. List the ten most interesting.**

1 Underline two phrases in the following sentence that tell you a. where the boy was and b. what Christa was worried about.

Christa shouldn't have worried about the bad-tempered boy beside her on the bus.

2 Say whether the clause underlined in the following sentence is a subordinate or a main clause:

Jack walked slowly towards the locked door <u>although he had been warned against it</u>.

Relative clauses

A **relative clause** is a type of subordinate clause (see pages 12–13). Relative clauses start with a relative pronoun (see pages 14–15) – **that**, **which**, **whose**, **who**, **where** or **when** – which refers back to the noun.

We use **who** for people, **which** for things and **that** for people or things.

Look at these two sentences below on the left. They could be written as one sentence, using a relative clause (see below on the right).

There's Jack. He lives next door.	noun / relative clause There's Jack, **who** lives next door. relative pronoun – refers back to Jack

Look at these examples:

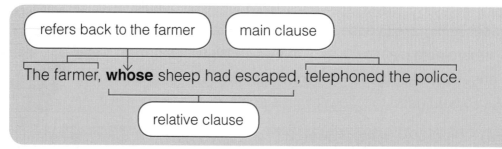

refers back to the farmer / main clause

The farmer, **whose** sheep had escaped, telephoned the police.

relative clause

refers back to the book The book **that** was signed by the author was a best-seller.	refers back to the hospital The hospital **where** I was born has been extended.
refers back to the day It was a day **when** everything went wrong!	refers back to the award Sonia won a special award, **which** was presented in assembly.

Keyword

Relative clause ➤ A subordinate clause introduced by a relative pronoun

Dropping the relative pronoun

Sometimes a relative pronoun can be dropped from the start of the relative clause and still make sense.

The cake **that was sitting on the table** was chocolate.

or

The cake **sitting on the table** was chocolate.

The teacher, **who was firm but fair**, was very popular.

or

The teacher, **firm but fair**, was very popular.

But in this sentence, **whose** cannot be dropped:

The dog, **whose** owner was at work, was bored.

Take care when omitting the relative pronoun – you might need to make changes to the wording! For example: **The girl who lives next door is ten**. This cannot become **The girl lives next door is ten**; it would need to be changed to: **The girl living next door is ten**.

Listen up 11

Have a go! Find an example of a relative clause beginning with each of the relative pronouns <u>who</u>, <u>whose</u>, <u>that</u> and <u>which</u>.

Test yourself

① Rewrite each sentence so that it contains a relative clause introduced by a relative pronoun. You will need to add some more words so that your sentence makes sense.

a. My neighbour, old and unsteady, needs help in his garden.

b. The kite, brightly coloured, danced on the breeze.

c. My dog, Benji, is very giddy.

Creating Sentences

Statements

A **statement** is a sentence that contains some information. It usually ends in a full stop.

Our school has two playing fields**.**

Dominic is ten and likes rugby**.**

Questions

A **question** asks something and always ends with a question mark.

What time are you coming home**?**

Why do dogs wag their tails**?**

How is your mother**?**

Where have you been**?**

Did you ever read that book I told you about**?**

Have you heard what happened to Amer yesterday**?**

Listen up 12

Keywords

Statement ➤ A sentence that gives information

Question ➤ A sentence that asks something

Commands

A **command** is a sentence telling someone to do something. It ends either in a full stop or an exclamation mark. A command uses verbs which command or instruct us to do something.

Eat your dinner now! 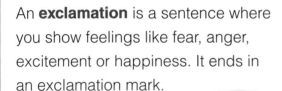 command **Tell** me your name, please.

Exclamations

An **exclamation** is a sentence where you show feelings like fear, anger, excitement or happiness. It ends in an exclamation mark.

What a long day it has been!

How sad I was when my sister broke her arm!

What a surprise I had when I opened the door!

What a lot of presents there are under the tree!

How lovely Mum's flowers look in that vase!

How wonderful it would be to fly to the moon!

Keywords

Command ➤ A sentence that gives an instruction

Exclamation ➤ A sentence that shows feelings like fear, anger, happiness or excitement

Top tip!

The noun **exclamation** comes from the verb **exclaim**. This should help you remember that an exclamation is followed by an exclamation mark!

Have a go!

Using command verbs, write a set of instructions for making your favourite breakfast.

Test yourself

❶ Write a question for each of the following statements:

a. Horses eat hay.

b. Australia is in the Southern Hemisphere.

c. I go to bed at 9.00 pm.

Creating Sentences

This mind map will help you remember all the main points from this topic. Have a go at drawing your own mind map.

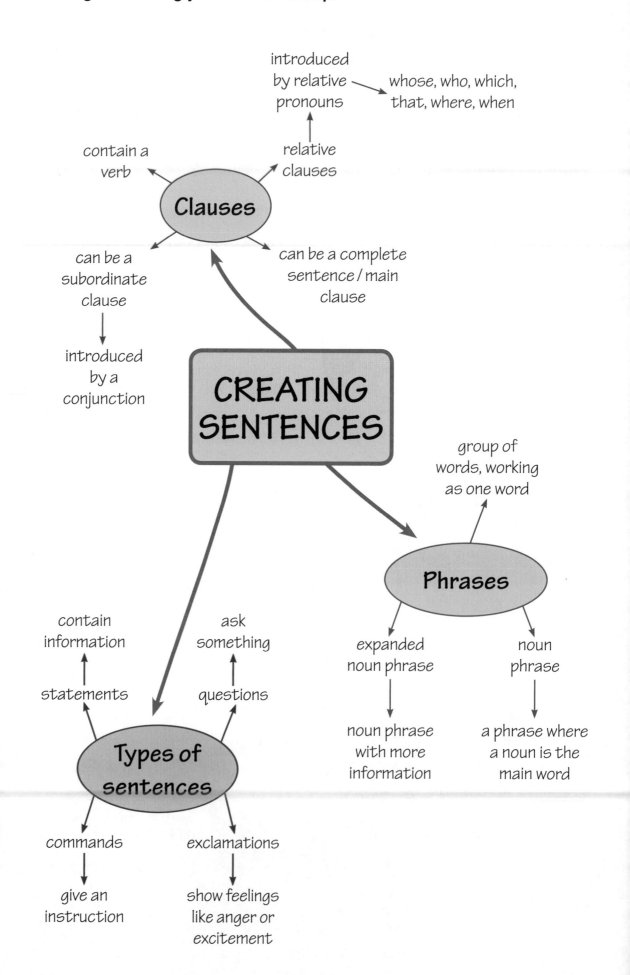

introduced by relative pronouns → whose, who, which, that, where, when

contain a verb

relative clauses

Clauses

can be a subordinate clause

can be a complete sentence / main clause

introduced by a conjunction

CREATING SENTENCES

group of words, working as one word

Phrases

expanded noun phrase

noun phrase

noun phrase with more information

a phrase where a noun is the main word

contain information

ask something

statements

questions

Types of sentences

commands

exclamations

give an instruction

show feelings like anger or excitement

1 Add determiners and adjectives to make expanded noun phrases: **(4 marks)**

a. .... rabbit   **c.** .... teachers

b. .... funfair   **d.** .... butterfly

2 Underline the phrase containing a preposition that shows the boy is being careful. **(1 mark)**

Sam scrambled with great caution over the rocks.

3 Tick the box for each sentence to show whether the text in bold is a main clause or a subordinate clause. **(3 marks)**

Sentence	Main clause	Subordinate clause
Although it was almost home time, **the teacher began a new chapter of the book**.		
As they were expecting friends, **James and Jules tidied their rooms**.		
Stella forgot to hand in her library book **because she was in a hurry to get home**.		

4 Write a relative pronoun in each gap. **(3 marks)**

a. The homework, ... we all found difficult, is due in first thing in the morning.

b. My Aunty Vivienne, ... came to tea yesterday, has been taken to hospital.

c. The school caretaker, ... shed was destroyed by vandals, still has a smile on her face.

5 Tick the box to show the type of sentence. **(4 marks)**

Sentence	Statement	Question	Command	Exclamation
Erin, finish brushing your teeth now!				
How much longer until we arrive?				
I have just bought a new bike.				
How silly my little brother is at times!				

6 Choose an appropriate subordinating conjunction to join these clauses together: **(4 marks)**

a. My aunty is coming for tea later. .... It's my mum's birthday.

b. You can't go out. .... It is raining so heavily.

c. We can't get into school. .... The caretaker opens the door.

d. We were told to stand at the back of the classroom. .... It wasn't actually us who had been talking.

Subject

The **subject** of a sentence is the person or thing that is 'doing' or 'being'. The subject is usually a noun, a pronoun or a noun phrase.

> **People** often go to the seaside on sunny days.

The subject is the collective noun **people**.

> **Sadie** enjoys having an ice-cream.

The subject is the proper noun **Sadie**.

> **It** cools her down in the heat.

The subject is the pronoun **it**.

> **The sea** is so refreshing!

The subject is the noun phrase **the sea**.

 **Top tip!** To help you find the subject in a sentence, find the verb and see who or what is doing something.

 **Listen up 13**

Keyword

Subject ➤ The person or thing 'doing' or 'being' something in the sentence.

 **Parent tip!** **You** is the same word in both singular and plural; both agree with the same verb form. It is the **context** that tells us whether it is singular **you** or plural **you**.

Subject–Verb agreement

Every clause or sentence has a verb and a subject.

It is important that the subject agrees with the verb.

Where the subject is singular, the verb must be in the singular form so it **agrees** with the subject.

Where the subject is plural, the verb must be in the plural form so it **agrees** with the subjects.

---

singular subject

Thomas does his homework every night.

singular verb

---

singular subject

The weather is cold and frosty.

singular verb

---

plural subject

The brothers do their homework every night.

plural verb

---

singular or plural subject

You don't have enough money.

singular or plural verb

Write the correct form of to jump for each personal pronoun:

I, you, he/she/it, we, they.

Test yourself

❶ Rewrite the sentences so that the subjects agree with the verbs, then underline the subjects.

a. The children is dancing to the music.

b. You has been very well-behaved today.

c. Running down the road were a herd of cows.

d. I does my homework every night.

Subject and object

Some sentences have one **subject** with an agreeing verb. For example:

They are running.

Others will include an **object**. The object is the noun, pronoun or noun phrase that comes after the verb. It shows what the subject is 'acting upon'. Some verbs don't have objects, for example: The genie **disappeared**.

Noun as the object

These are example sentences where a noun is the object.

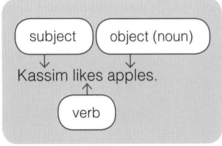

subject   object (noun)

Kassim likes apples.

verb

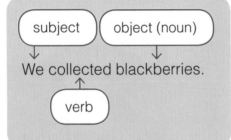

subject   object (noun)

We collected blackberries.

verb

Top tip!

The object shows what the subject and verb are 'acting on'. Ask yourself: what did Kassim eat? (apples!), what did we collect? (blackberries!).

Listen up 14

Keywords

Subject ➤ The person or thing that is doing or being something in the sentence

Object ➤ A noun, pronoun or noun phrase showing what the subject is acting upon

Noun phrase and expanded noun phrase as the object

These sentences below are examples where the noun phrase is the object.

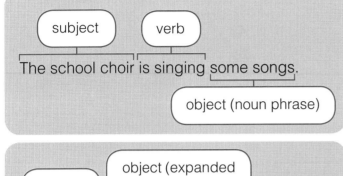

The school choir is singing some songs.

- subject
- verb
- object (noun phrase)

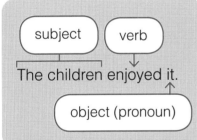

She ran the 200m race in record time.

- subject
- object (expanded noun phrase)
- verb

Pronoun as the object

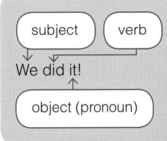

The children enjoyed it.

- subject
- verb
- object (pronoun)

We did it!

- subject
- verb
- object (pronoun)

Search through your reading book for examples of clauses with a subject and an object. Is the object a noun, noun phrase, expanded noun phrase or pronoun?

Test yourself

1 Underline the subject and circle the object in these sentences:

a. My dog gnawed his bone.

b. We all told him not to run!

c. Flooding is damaging many homes.

d. The weather announcer presented a temperature graph.

Active voice

Most writing is in the **active voice**. Writing in the active voice just means that the subject of the sentence is doing something and the object (if there is one) of the sentence is what the subject is 'acting upon'.

Subject	Verb	Object
We	threw	some snowballs.
Ben	saw	the postman.

Ask yourself who or what is the subject 'acting upon'?
What were we throwing?
Who did Ben see?

Passive voice

Where the subject is unknown or we want to put the attention on the person or thing affected by the action, we use the **passive voice**. We can change an active voice sentence to the passive voice by making the object the subject.

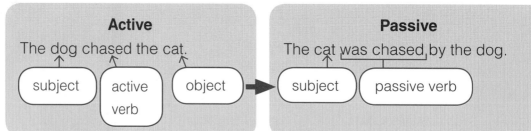

Sometimes, the object – the thing doing the action – isn't included in the sentence.

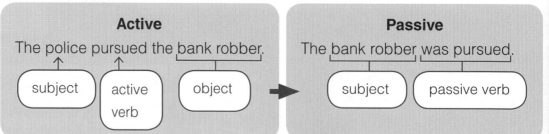

In the passive voice sentence, the bank robber still isn't doing the action; the action is 'being done' to him even though we are not told by whom.

Keywords

Active voice ➤ When the subject of the sentence is doing or being something; the object is having it done to them / it

Passive voice ➤ When the subject isn't carrying out the action but is being acted upon by someone or something

Top tip! You will often see the passive voice being used in formal speech and writing: For example: **I have been most warmly welcomed to this assembly by the Head Teacher**.

Parent tip! Spot the passive voice!
Look for the combination of the verb **to be** + the **past tense** of the verb:
She **was attacked** (by the bees).
She **is being praised** (by her teacher).

Listen up **15**

Have a go! Turn this short paragraph from the active voice to the passive voice:

The teacher warned us not to hand our homework in late. She had reminded us many times before. The Head Teacher was definitely going to tell us off now!

Test yourself

① Say whether the following sentences are in the active or passive voice:

a. The children were swiftly rescued.

b. The older children pulled the youngest to safety first.

c. Everyone climbed onto the bus.

d. Some children were driven home by their parents.

Direct speech

When we want to tell the reader the exact words spoken by someone, we use **inverted commas** to show the beginning and the end of what they are saying.

This is known as **direct speech**. Sometimes inverted commas are called **speech marks**.

We will be looking at how to use these accurately on pages 48–49.

"I'm sure I've met you somewhere before," said Toby to the old gentleman.

"Let me see – wasn't it last winter during the bad snowfall?" replied Mr Bates.

"I'll be back to help you with the gardening later!" called Dad.

Under her breath, Mum muttered, "Later… when it's going to be raining."

Sometimes we want to report what has been said rather than use direct speech.

My brother said that he had hidden Mum's present under his bed.

"I've hidden Mum's present under my bed," said my brother.

Note that the verb tense and subject changes in the direct speech.

he had hidden ⟶ **I have** hidden

| Past perfect tense | Present perfect tense |

Using different verbs

There are many different verbs you can use to show the way in which the subject speaks in direct speech.

muttered	croaked	whispered	coughed
stuttered	screeched	agreed	admitted
uttered	shrieked	queried	begged
sighed	called	signalled	barked
cried	shouted	pointed	bellowed

Keywords

Inverted commas/Speech marks ➤ Used on either side of a sentence, phrase or word to show that someone is speaking

Direct speech ➤ A sentence in inverted commas showing the exact words spoken by someone

Top tip! If you are using speech bubbles in a storyboard, or writing a play, you do not need to use inverted commas.

Have a go! Read a newspaper article and identify one example of direct speech and one example of reported speech (where someone reports what someone else has said).

Test yourself

① Turn these sentences, where we are told what was said, into direct speech:

a. The Head Teacher told his staff that there would be no school due to the heavy snow.

b. My mum said I should get my homework done immediately or there would be no TV.

c. The traffic warden grumbled that we had parked on double yellow lines.

d. My swimming instructor said that I was ready to take my diving badge.

Informal speech and writing

We use **informal speech** when we are chatting to, texting or emailing our friends and family. It is a relaxed way of speaking where we might use **slang**, **abbreviations** and **colloquialisms**. We might also use incorrect grammar such as "we done" instead of "we did".

Hey, how's it going? You goin' to footie practice?

Nah, can't be bothered. Got loadsa homework and Mum'll kill me if I get into more diffs with me maths.

We use informal writing when writing a postcard or a diary entry.

Fri. 9th Sept.

What an amazing day! Just chilled with Freya and Brogan then grabbed a pizza for tea. Think we'll head to the park tomorrow and hang out with Cassie and her crowd. It's gonna be wicked and I totally can't wait!

Keywords

Informal speech and writing ➤ A relaxed, chatty way of speaking and writing used with family and friends

Slang ➤ Very informal speech used among friends

Abbreviations ➤ Shortened word forms

Colloquialisms ➤ Expressions in informal, everyday language

Standard English ➤ Using the rules of English correctly

Formal speech ➤ Speaking and writing using correct grammar and vocabulary

Subjunctive ➤ A verb form that shows a wish or an imaginary state

Formal speech and writing

We should use **Standard English** in **formal speech**. This means using correct grammar. We should use Standard English when talking with our teachers and other adults beyond our family and close circle of friends. When delivering a speech, the language should also be more formal.

Sometimes when using formal speech or writing we use the **subjunctive** form of verbs. Often the subjunctive is used in a subordinate clause:

> subjunctive form of verb 'to be'
> ↓
> If you **were** to hear the fire alarm, please follow the signs to the emergency exits at the rear of the hall.

The subjunctive can be used to show a wish or imaginary state:

> I wish I **were** a fly on the wall.

> I wish I **were** a million miles from here!

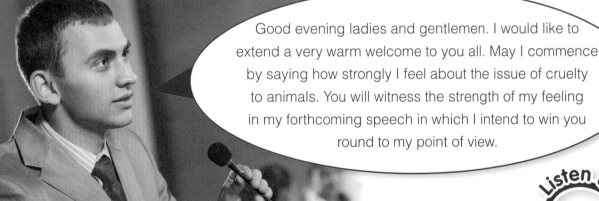

Good evening ladies and gentlemen. I would like to extend a very warm welcome to you all. May I commence by saying how strongly I feel about the issue of cruelty to animals. You will witness the strength of my feeling in my forthcoming speech in which I intend to win you round to my point of view.

Listen up
17

Have a go!
Listen to the news then listen to a popular soap on the TV; how does the speech in each differ?

Test yourself

❶ Rewrite these sentences in Standard English:

a. The head's gotta give us a snow day!

b. It's at least, like, a metre deep and me mum's car's broke.

c. OK, see what happens but I am so not goin' in!

This mind map will help you remember all the main points from this topic. Have a go at drawing your own mind map.

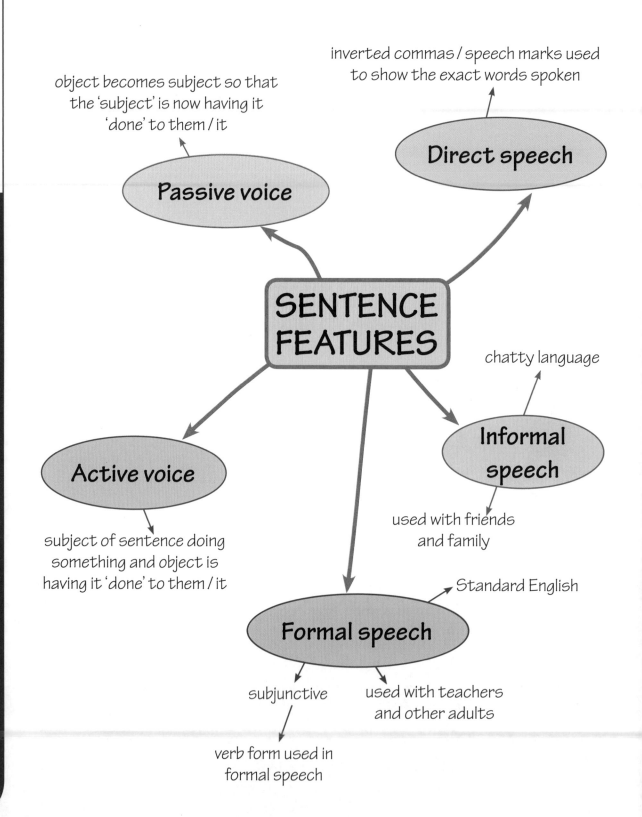

object becomes subject so that the 'subject' is now having it 'done' to them / it

inverted commas / speech marks used to show the exact words spoken

Passive voice

Direct speech

SENTENCE FEATURES

chatty language

Informal speech

used with friends and family

Active voice

subject of sentence doing something and object is having it 'done' to them / it

Standard English

Formal speech

subjunctive

used with teachers and other adults

verb form used in formal speech

1 Write the correct verb form to agree with the subject in these sentences.

  a. You goes to the cinema every Saturday. .... **(1 mark)**

  b. We was hoping to finish early today. .... **(1 mark)**

  c. I seen a massive spider. .... **(1 mark)**

2 Turn these passive voice sentences into the active voice.

  a. The puppy was persuaded by the children to stop eating the toy.

  (1 mark)

  ....

  b. We were asked by our teachers to submit two more pieces of work.

  (1 mark)

  ....

  c. The children had been lifted to safety by the firemen so they were
  out of danger. **(1 mark)**

  ....

3 Write the subjects and objects you find in these three sentences into the
correct column in the table. **(3 marks)**

  Ciara approached the cliff, feeling rather nervous. She could hear
  the crashing waves below. Suddenly a bird swooped down and brushed
  her hair.

	Subjects	Objects
1	....	....
2	....	....
3	....	....

4 Change the following formal sentences to informal; use your dictionary to
help with tricky words.

  We are required to depart at 7.00 pm precisely. If anyone is tardy, there
  will be repercussions. We must ensure the highest levels of confidentiality
  are adhered to. **(2 marks)**

  ....

  ....

  ....

5 Turn these sentences into direct speech, taking care to punctuate accurately.

  a. The referee said that Sarah had played brilliantly in defence. **(1 mark)**

  ....

  b. Our parents explained that the holiday we liked the best was out of our
  price range. **(1 mark)**

  ....

Punctuation

Punctuation marks are 'signposts' that help us understand a text, whether we are reading silently or aloud. Without them, it could be very difficult to understand what the writer means and we might get rather breathless as we wouldn't know when to make a pause or a stop!

Look at this extract where the punctuation is missing:

> guy looking very suspicious turned round only to be confronted by the head with a frosty stare she invited him to step into her office guy nervously went in

Is it a person called Guy or is the writer talking about a 'guy' but without a determiner? Is he confronted by a 'head' – in other words, is this a horror story? – or a Head Teacher? Does the 'head' have a frosty stare or is it the Head Teacher who has the frosty stare?

Here is the extract with punctuation inserted:

> Guy, looking very suspicious, turned round only to be confronted by the Head. With a frosty stare, she invited him to step into her office. Guy nervously went in.

Capital letters and full stops

From an early age we are taught to start our sentences with a **capital letter** and end with a **full stop**. Sometimes, we get so involved in our writing that we forget one or both of these! Capital letters are not just used at the start of a sentence though – we know we have to use them for proper nouns too (see pages 4–5). And of course a sentence can end in a question mark or an exclamation mark (see pages 28–29).

| capital letter to start sentence | capital letter for proper noun |

Despite a distinct lack of full stops in **C**harlie's writing, with the **H**ead **T**eacher's support she got there in the end.

| capital letter for title | full stop at end of sentence |

Question marks

Question marks come at the end of a question – you do not need a full stop as well because it replaces the full stop. You only ever need one question mark in your writing.

> Why don't you come out to play**?**

Make sure your capital letter **looks like** a capital letter – it needs to be taller than the lower case letters in your sentence and should not join.

Top tip!

Exclamation marks

Exclamation marks come at the end of an exclamation or command. These can express shock, anger, surprise or delight. An exclamation mark replaces the full stop – and you only need one! It's tempting in story writing to use two or three to intensify the drama but it's not necessary.

> What a wild thunderstorm that is**!**   exclamation

> How naughty you have been today**!**   exclamation

> How lovely it is to see you at last**!**   exclamation

> Get upstairs to your room now**!**   command

Keywords

Punctuation marks ➤ 'Signposts' to help us understand text.
Capital letters ➤ Letters in upper case, used at the start of sentences and proper nouns
Full stop ➤ Punctuation mark at the end of a sentence
Question mark ➤ Punctuation mark at the end of a question
Exclamation mark ➤ Punctuation mark at the end of an exclamation or command

How would you explain to an alien what punctuation is and what it is for?

Have a go!

Test yourself

❶ Insert the missing capital letters, full stops, question marks and exclamation marks in the following sentences:

a. what was the score

b. what an amazing match that was

c. i can't wait to phone uncle eric do you think he'll be home from work

Punctuation

Commas can be used in different ways, for example:

- to separate items in a list
- to show a brief pause in a sentence to make the meaning clearer and avoid **ambiguity**
- in direct speech
- to separate a clause or phrase from the rest of the sentence
- to separate an adverbial from the rest of the sentence.

We will look at another way we can use commas on page 53.

Listen up
19

Keyword

Ambiguity ➤ Having more than one meaning

Commas in lists

Our holiday clothes included: sandals, shorts, sun-hats, sun-cream and swimming costumes.

Notice there is no comma after sun-cream, before the word **and**.

Commas to show a pause to clarify meaning and avoid ambiguity

The meaning of a sentence can change completely if a comma is in the wrong place or missed out.

"Let's eat Granny!"   is quite different to   "Let's eat, Granny!"

Parent tip!

When reading something out from a paper to your child, say the word **comma** when one appears to reinforce why we use them.

Commas in direct speech

Where direct speech is followed by **said** or a similar word, there should be a comma (or exclamation mark or question mark) before the final inverted commas.

> "Today we should make a snowman**,**" decided Jamie.

If the word **said** or a similar word comes **before** the speech, a comma should come after it and before the **opening** inverted commas.

> Brogan quickly replied**,** "I have a carrot for the nose and some coal for the eyes."

Commas to separate

Commas are used to separate a clause or phrase from the rest of the sentence.

> Even though it was raining**,** Jack went to play outside.
>
> comma between initial subordinate clause and main clause

> The naughty dog**,** who had been playing manically all day**,** was finally asleep.
>
> commas before and after the relative clause

> Without explanation**,** Mia left the classroom and didn't return.
>
> comma after the introductory phrase

Have a go! Read aloud from your book or a newspaper, leaving out the commas. Do the sentences still make sense? Are you a little breathless from the lack of pauses?

Test yourself

❶ Insert the missing commas in the following text:

Douglas and Emily who were brother and sister were going camping for the weekend. Between them they packed: sleeping bags jumpers walking boots a Thermos flask snacks and a camera.

Inverted commas in direct speech

Inverted commas are sometimes called speech marks. We use them to show the start and end of spoken words. When you are reading, you will notice that some authors use double inverted commas "" and others use single ''. When more than one person is speaking, we call it a **dialogue**.

> "I have just about had enough of that pup," said Jamie's mum.
>
> His dad replied, "Well, you were the one who really wanted a dog."

Make sure your inverted commas are not too big; they need to be on the same level as any capital or tall letters in the speech. They must come **after** the final punctuation mark, whether it's a comma, full stop, exclamation mark or question mark.

> „My brother and I are both keen astrologers", Mia told her teacher. ✗
>
> "My brother and I are both keen astrologers," Mia told her teacher. ✓

Inverted commas for quotations

Sometimes in a reading comprehension exercise you are asked to use quotations to support your answers.

> Here in the deep silence of the sleeping country, the only things that went by were the trains. They seemed to be all that was left to link the children to the old life that had once been theirs.

Q: Quoting directly from the text, what tells the reader that the trains were a connection to the children's past?

A: The author uses the phrase "old life" to show that the trains were a "link" to the lives they led before they came to the countryside.

Keyword

Dialogue ➤ A conversation between two or more people

Inverted commas for nicknames and other titles

Sometimes inverted commas are used to show a nickname, so that the reader knows this isn't the person's real name.

> I call my little brother "The Destroyer" because he runs around like a whirlwind.

We might find inverted commas used to show we are talking about a book, film or play title.

> Last night we were lucky enough to see "The Lion King" at the theatre.

Top tip! Get them the right way around! Your opening inverted commas should look like back-to-front commas and your closing inverted commas should look like normal commas.

Parent tip! Help your child to form inverted commas that are appropriate to the size of their handwriting.

Have a go! Choose a novel where there is plenty of dialogue and copy down an example of speech that ends with a comma, question mark, exclamation mark and full stop. Make sure that your final inverted commas come <u>after</u> these punctuation marks.

Test yourself

① Add inverted commas and other missing punctuation into the correct positions in this dialogue:

> There really isn't much point in packing a picnic said Joe
>
> Well, it's not going to rain forever replied Dylan Look over there – I can see a patch of blue sky
>
> Good for you Joe said grumpily Do you really think that means the sun will come out

An **apostrophe** looks like a comma but does not sit on the line – it sits at the same height as inverted commas.

We can use it in two different ways:

- to show **possession** – in other words, to show that something belongs to someone
- to show **omission**, where a letter, or letters, has/have been left out – in other words, **contraction**, where a word, or words, has/have been made shorter.

Apostrophes for possession

The rules for using an apostrophe to show possession are:

- singular nouns – add an apostrophe after the word followed by an **s**
- plural nouns ending in **s** – add only an apostrophe after the final **s**
- proper nouns ending in **s** – add an apostrophe followed by an **s**.

> apostrophe after lady (singular noun) followed by **s**

The lady's handbag was found by the police after they had found **the thieves' footsteps** in the mud.

> apostrophe after the **s** in thieves (plural noun)

The lady's handbag = the handbag belonging to the lady

the thieves' footsteps = the footsteps belonging to the thieves

There's an important exception to the possession rule! The word **it's** always means **it is**, so for possession it does **not** get an apostrophe.
The dog wagged **its** tail. ✓
Top tip! If it was **it's**, the sentence would read:
The dog wagged **it is** tail. ✗ which doesn't make sense at all!

Apostrophes for contraction or omission

When we speak or write informally, we often use contractions. These are words that have been shortened by removing a letter or letters; the letter or letters has/have been omitted so we sometimes refer to this as omission.

The following are common contractions:

I am	I'm
she is	she's
we have	we've

they are	they're
does not	doesn't
will not	won't

cannot	can't
it is	it's
we will	we'll

It's important that you position the apostrophe in the correct place – where the missing letter or letters would be.

We will ↓   it is ↓

We'll have to remember **it's** Dad's birthday next week.
It'll be fun to surprise him, **'cause he's** bound to forget.
↑   ↑   ↑

It will   because   he is

Keywords

Apostrophe ➤ A punctuation mark used to show omission (contraction) or possession
Possession ➤ Ownership
Omission ➤ Leaving a letter or letters out
Contraction ➤ A word that has been made shorter

Parent tip!

If someone's name ends in **s**, such as James, an apostrophe followed by an **s** can be used in the normal way.
James's pens.
Words ending in double **s** such as **princess** follow the normal rule too.
The prince took the princess's hand.

Have a go!

Make a list of people's names on one side of your page then pair them up with items you can see around the house, showing possession. Sarah's lampshade, Chris's picture… etc.

Test yourself

❶ Insert the missing apostrophes in these sentences:

Jakes mums chicken pie wasnt the best. Shed burnt its edges as shed left it in the oven too long. They shouldve gone out to Charlies Chippy, thought Jake.

Parenthesis is a word or phrase inserted into a sentence as an explanation or afterthought. The word or phrase sits inside a pair of **brackets**, **dashes** or **commas**. When you take the words in **parentheses** out of the sentence, what is left still makes sense.

Brackets

Brackets can come in the middle of a sentence or at the end.

> We ate the stale cake and said our goodbyes (we wouldn't be going back there again).

> The children (who have only been swimming for a couple of years) did two lengths in the charity swim.

> It was only eight o'clock (I know because I looked at my watch), yet the town was in complete darkness.

Top tip! Use dashes, commas and brackets in your writing to show parenthesis. It will make it more interesting to read.

Dashes

Dashes, another form of parenthesis, do the same job as brackets.
A dash is twice the length of a hyphen (see page 56). There needs to be two dashes to use them in parenthesis. We will look at using single dashes on page 55.

> The teachers were very cross – not surprisingly – and spoke to the whole school about poor behaviour.

> Finding a way across the swollen river – difficult even on a calm day – was proving almost impossible.

Commas

Commas can also be used to show parenthesis.

> While we were on holiday, the Browns, a family we met over there, helped us put up our tent.

The words in parentheses give us extra information. They are often relative clauses with the relative pronoun left out.

> While we were on holiday, the Browns, **who were a family we met over there**, helped us put up our tent.

> Marco, **tightrope walker extraordinaire**, amazed the crowd with his daring agility.

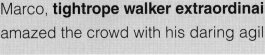

Help your child to use parenthesis – and to remember the word – when supporting their writing.

"Why don't you put those words in parentheses?" "What parentheses could you use here?"

Keywords

Parenthesis ➤ A word or phrase inserted into a sentence as an explanation or afterthought

Brackets, dashes and commas ➤ Can show parenthesis

Parentheses ➤ The punctuation marks used to indicate parenthesis

Have a go!

Insert suitable parentheses in this sentence:

We went white-water rafting an often dangerous sport and thoroughly enjoyed ourselves.

Test yourself

① Rewrite these sentences, inserting a word, phrase or clause in the gaps, using appropriate parentheses:

a. I couldn't be bothered to go swimming .... so I stayed at home.

b. We were amazed by the trapeze artists at the circus ....

c. Having been there on holiday before .... we knew our way around.

Colons

Colons can be used in different ways:

- after a clause, to introduce another clause that explains or gives more detail
- to introduce a list (as here!)
- instead of a comma, before a quotation
- in play scripts to show where a character's lines begin.

> Finding the answer wasn't easy**:** first, I had to unravel the mysterious clue left in the garden.

> The headline said**:** "Children Grasping Grammar is Great!"

> Juliet**:** O Romeo, Romeo, wherefore art thou Romeo?
> Romeo**:** [Aside] Shall I hear more, or shall I speak at this?

Listen up
23

Semi-colons

Semi-colons can be used in different ways:

- to link two closely related sentences instead of using a full stop
- to separate items in a list where some items might be longer than one or two words.

> I have been going to the Lake District for years; I love the spectacular views.

> Our class recently conducted a school dinner survey: thirty percent of children wanted bigger portions; twenty five percent wanted fizzy drinks; thirty five percent wanted more choice and the rest thought things were good as they were.

Keywords

Colon ➤ Introduces a clause that gives detail or introduces a list, a quotation or speech in a play script

Semi-colon ➤ Links two closely related sentences or separates items in a list where some items might be longer than one or two words

Dash ➤ A single dash shows a break or pause in a sentence

Bullet points ➤ Used to draw attention to items in a list

Dashes

A single **dash** is used to show a break or pause in a sentence. Often it can be used to add suspense or it might show a change of direction in the sentence. Sometimes a dash can replace a comma, semi-colon, or colon.

> We had reached the top of Everest – or had we?

> When we finally clambered to the top, we fell into each other's arms – now we could celebrate.

Bullet points

Bullet points are used to draw the reader's attention to important information. The information is given in a list going down the page. Bullet points usually come after a sentence ending with a colon. The text following the bullet points does not need to start with a capital letter or end with a full stop if it is not a full sentence.

 **Top tip!** Don't make bullet points like footballs in your writing! They should be obvious but not huge! They should line up one below the other.

> At school today we did the following:
> - science in the woodland area
> - cooking in the kitchen
> - PE in the hall.

> At the meeting it was decided that:
> - All children must wear regulation school uniform at all times.
> - Parents should ensure that children do not wear earrings.
> - Watches can be worn as long as they don't beep in lessons.

 **Have a go!**

Write a definition of – and the rules for using – bullet points using... bullet points!

Test yourself

1. Insert a semi-colon, a dash, a colon or bullet points in the correct place in these sentences.

   a. My father and I play football at the weekend he is the goalkeeper and I am the striker.

   b. We turned the corner and there it was a wild-eyed creature, foaming at the mouth.

   c. The ingredients are flour, eggs, milk and sugar.

Hyphens

Hyphens can be used in different ways:

- in some **compound words** (two words joined together)
- to join prefixes to some words
- to show word breaks at the end of a line.

Hyphenated compound words:

| up-to-date | kind-hearted | quick-thinking | accident-prone | self-service |

Joining prefixes to other words:

| co-ordinate | re-establish | re-present | co-owner | co-operative |

We sometimes use a hyphen when joining a prefix ending with a vowel to another word starting with a vowel, although you will often see **coordinate** and **cooperate** rather than **co-ordinate** and **co-operate**.

For other words, joining the prefix with a hyphen avoids confusion of meaning, for example: re-cover, 'to put a new cover on something', and recover, 'to get well again'.

Showing word breaks:

Word breaks should come after a syllable. Never hyphenate one letter on its own. If you think you are going to struggle to get a final letter on the line, then do not break the word – instead go to the next line. It doesn't matter if there's a slight gap at the end of your line!

Dear Mum and Dad,

I'm having a great time on my residential trip but even so I'll look forward to getting back to my own bed.

Listen up 24

Keywords

Hyphen ➤ A punctuation mark that links words to make some compound words, to join prefixes to some words or to show a word break at the end of a line

Hyphenated compound words ➤ Two words combined with a hyphen to make one new word

Ellipsis ➤ Shows missing text

Ellipses

An **ellipsis** shows that a word, words, a sentence or sentences have been omitted (intentionally) from the text. It is often shown by three dots. Ellipses can be used in different ways.

Ellipsis used to avoid the need to copy out the whole text:

> For homework this week, please read page 55: "Roald Admundsen, a Norwegian, spent**...** an accident."

Ellipsis to show suspense:

> I crept further into the depths of the musty cellar until the creaking of a door hinge stopped me in my tracks**...**

Ellipsis to show an interruption:

> "But we never get to go to the beach any more at**...**"
> "Stop moaning, Sam," interrupted Tom. "We will go next half term."

Ellipsis to allow the reader to decide what is missing:

> As she waved goodbye to her friends, Suzi thought that would be the end of the whole saga; but there was always next time**...**

When reading a book, take note where words are hyphenated at the end of a line and sound out the syllable(s) up to the break.

How many examples of hyphenated compound words can you find in your reading book, comic or newspaper?

❶ What compound words can you make using a hyphen from the words below?

in	known	mad
tempered	law	well
brother	sport	bad

This mind map will help you remember all the main points from this topic.
Have a go at drawing your own mind map.

Punctuation

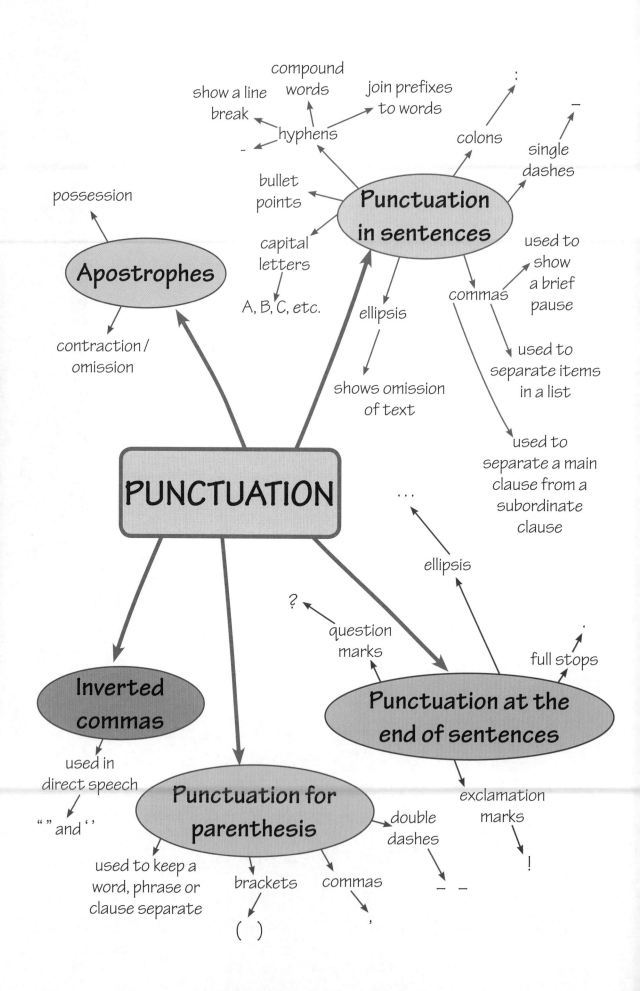

1 What does the term 'apostrophes for possession' mean? **(1 mark)**

....

....

2 Add the missing commas.

a. " We're going to eat Dad " said the hungry children. **(1 mark)**

b. The girls were looking forward to chicken potatoes peas and some cold juice. **(1 mark)**

c. The rescue boat a vessel the coastguards had been using for many years swiftly reached the canoe. **(1 mark)**

d. This school according to its website expects a high standard of behaviour. **(1 mark)**

3 Add a dash to the following sentence: **(1 mark)**

We've been looking at holidays we are thinking of Spain, France or Italy.

4 Add a semi-colon to the following sentence: **(1 mark)**

We are really leaning towards a trip to Spain we were there last summer.

5 Add a colon to the following sentence: **(1 mark)**

Other options for our holiday are the following Croatia, Portugal and Bulgaria.

6 What is the rule for hyphenating words at the end of a line? **(1 mark)**

....

....

7 Write a sentence to show that you know how to use a colon. **(1 mark)**

....

....

Synonyms

A **synonym** is a word with the same or similar meaning as another word. To avoid your writing being repetitive and boring, try to use synonyms to make it more interesting.

Read this paragraph.

> I was so **happy** when I saw that Sam's **happy** dog was sitting next to my own **happy dog** that I **sat** next to them.

Now read this paragraph using synonyms.

> I was so **delighted** to see that Sam's **contented** dog was sitting next to my own **cheerful canine friend** that I **plonked** myself beside them.

A synonym for 'said'

When story writing, it is easy to fall into the trap of over-using the word 'said', but think of all the different words you could use instead!

> "My word, you really are suffering with that cold!" **exclaimed** Mum.
>
> "I feel even worse than I did this morning," **spluttered** Fran.
>
> "Well, it's off to bed for you, young lady, and straight to sleep!" Mum **ordered**.

You do not always have to use a word for **said**; if it's obvious who is speaking, then vary your writing by leaving it out. In the examples above, you could leave out 'Mum ordered' because the dialogue is only between Mum and Fran so it's clear who is speaking!

Antonyms

An **antonym** is a word that is opposite in meaning to another word.

tall	short
full	empty

curly	straight
closed	open

Listen up 25

Parent tip! Encourage your child to use a **thesaurus** as well as a dictionary when writing.

Keywords

Synonym ➤ A word that means the same or almost the same as another word

Antonym ➤ A word that means the opposite to another word

Thesaurus ➤ A book of words and their synonyms

Top tip! Before you start story writing, build up a bank of synonyms for commons words such as **said**, **happy**, **sad** and **lovely**. Dip into it as you write.

Have a go! Read a newspaper article or an extract from a book and see how many synonyms you can find for the verbs, nouns and adjectives you come across.

Test yourself

① Create a table with two columns. Write the following words in the first column, then write antonyms for each in the second column.

sad

extrovert

exciting

stormy

Vocabulary and Spelling

A **prefix** is a string of letters added to the beginning of a word to turn it into another word. It does not change the spelling of the original word. Some prefixes change the word so that it is opposite or negative in meaning.

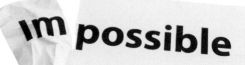

Prefixes dis and mis

The prefixes **dis** and **mis** usually give the word a negative meaning.

tasteful ⟶ **dis**tasteful

guided ⟶ **mis**guided

> I agreed with Claire but Katie **dis**agreed with us both.

Prefixes im and in

The prefixes **im** and **in** also give a negative meaning. If the **root word** starts with **m** or **p**, use **im**, but otherwise use **in**.

definite ⟶ **in**definite

perfect ⟶ **im**perfect

> Ben's art project was **in**complete; Tom, on the other hand, had finished his.

Prefixes il, ir and un

These prefixes also give an opposite meaning when placed in front of a word. If the root word starts with **l**, use the prefix **il**; if the root word starts with **r**, generally use **ir**.

legal ⟶ **il**legal (It would be very hard to say 'irlegal'!)

replaceable ⟶ **ir**replaceable (It would be quite hard to say 'ilreplaceable'!)

tie ⟶ **un**tie

Top tip!

Other prefixes include:
- **de**, which indicates removal or reversal (e.g. **de**compose).
- **over**, which can imply 'too much' (e.g. **over**run).
- **re**, which indicates 'again' or 'back' (e.g. **re**type, **re**wind).

Listen up 26

Prefixes from Latin and Greek

Some prefixes have their origins in Greek or Latin, such as **bi** meaning 'two', **tele** meaning 'far off' and **super** meaning 'greater or above'. With these, you just need to learn their meaning to help you work out the meaning of the whole word.

bi + cycle = bicycle	(two wheels)
tele + scope = telescope	(makes far off things appear closer)
super + market = supermarket	(a big shop)
anti + freeze = antifreeze	(prevents water freezing)
auto + biography = autobiography	(an account of someone's life, written by that person)

Keywords

Prefix ➤ A string of letters added to the start of a word to change its meaning

Root word ➤ A word in its own right, without a prefix or a suffix

Top tip!

Make the link to the number two when you come across words starting with the prefix **bi**, for example: binoculars, biannual, bilingual.

Have a go!

What do the prefixes <u>auto</u> and <u>aqua</u> mean? Write some words starting with these prefixes and write their meanings. Use these to help you to figure out what the prefixes mean.

Test yourself

❶ Unravel these anagrams to find words starting with <u>il</u> or <u>ir</u>.

a. sister liberi

b. little aire

c. rail ration

d. glaci olli

A **suffix** is a letter or a string of letters added to the end of a root word, changing or adding to its meaning.

Suffixes s and es

The suffix **s** can be added to most nouns to form the plural.

dog ⟶ dog**s**

If the noun ends in **ch**, **sh**, **ss** or **x**, the suffix **es** is added.

church ⟶ church**es**

wish ⟶ wish**es**

kiss ⟶ kiss**es**

fox ⟶ fox**es**

Suffixes able and ably

You can add **able** to a root word to make an adjective.
If the word ends in **ce** or **ge**, you need to keep the **e** when you add the suffix.

change ⟶ change**able**

The weather could change today. ⟶ The weather is looking quite chang**eable** today.

You can add **ably** to a root word to make an adverb.

considerable ⟶ consider**ably**

There is a considerable amount of litter in the park. ⟶ The litter in the park has got consider**ably** worse.

Suffixes ible and ibly

You can add **ible** to a root word to make an adjective.

sense ⟶ sens**ible**

That rabbit has no sense. ⟶ That rabbit isn't sens**ible**.

You can add **ibly** to a root word to make an adverb.

possible ⟶ poss**ibly**

There's no such thing as a 'poss', so watch out – some words do not have an obvious root because they come from other languages, such as Latin or Greek.

Keyword

Suffix ➤ A letter or a string of letters added to the root word to change or add to its meaning

Support your child to make connections with other words that have the Greek suffixes **logy**, **phone**, **phobia** and **meter**.

Suffixes from Greek

The suffixes **logy**, **phone**, **phobia** and **meter** have their origins in the Greek language.

zoology   telephone   claustrophobia   perimeter

Use a dictionary or the Internet to find out the meanings of the Greek suffixes <u>meter</u> and <u>phobia</u>.

Have a go!

Test yourself

❶ Add <u>able</u> and <u>ably</u> to the following words:

a. rely

b. desire

❷ Add <u>ible</u> and <u>ibly</u> to the following words:

a. audio

b. vision

Suffixes cial and tial

The suffixes **cial** and **tial** can be added to root words to make adjectives. The suffix **cial** is mainly used after a vowel and the suffix **tial** after a consonant.

office ⟶ offi**cial**
essence ⟶ essen**tial**

"Spatial" is an exception: can you think of any others?

Suffixes cious and tious

The suffixes **cious** and **tious** can also be used to make adjectives. The suffix **cious** is usually used if the root word ends in **ce**. If the word ends in **tion**, then the suffix **tious** is used.

grace ⟶ gra**cious**
caution ⟶ cau**tious**

The suffixes **ful** and **less** can also be used to form adjectives, e.g.
hope ⟶ hope**ful**
care ⟶ care**less**

Top tip!

Suffixes ence and ance

The suffixes **ence** and **ance** are used to make nouns. It is easy to misspell words with these suffixes because the sound they make at the end is not emphasised, or stressed, so both of these final syllables sound very similar.

- Use the suffix **ance** if a related word has an **ay** sound after the root word.

    observ**a**tion ⟶ observ**ance**

- If there is a related word with an **eh** sound after the root word, use **ence**.

    confid**e**nt ⟶ confid**ence**

- If a noun is formed from a verb that ends in **y**, **ure** or **ear**, then the ending of the noun will often be **ance**.

    disapp**ear** ⟶ disappear**ance**

- If a noun is formed from a verb ending in **ere** or **er**, then the ending will often be **ence**.

    inter**fere** ⟶ interfer**ence**

Remember to delete the final **y** before adding the suffix **ance**.

Top tip!

Suffixes ment, ness and er

The suffixes **ment**, **ness** and **er** can be used to form nouns.

enjoy ⟶ enjoy**ment**

happy ⟶ happi**ness**

teach ⟶ teach**er**

Suffixes ate, ise and ify

The suffixes **ate**, **ise** and **ify** can be used to convert nouns or adjectives into verbs.

participant ⟶ particip**ate**

agony ⟶ agon**ise**

solid ⟶ solid**ify**

How would you write the verbs 'interfere' and 'prefer' as nouns?

1 Add either <u>cial</u> or <u>tial</u> to the following words, remembering to apply the rule.

a. residence

b. face

c. sacrifice

d. influence

2 Use either <u>ence</u> or <u>ance</u> to turn these words into nouns:

a. adhere

b. rely

The rule 'i before e except after c, but only when it rhymes with bee'

Where the sound after a **soft c** is **ee**, the spelling is **ei** in accordance with the rule 'i before e except after c':

> deceit
> receipt
> deceive

There are of course some exceptions.

- Some words have an **ei** spelling, despite not coming after a **soft c**; they have an **ay** sound.

> eight
> weight
> beige

- Other words have an **ei** spelling but an **ee** sound.

> weird
> protein
> caffeine

Otherwise, you will find that words follow the rule **i before e**.

> piece
> field
> shield

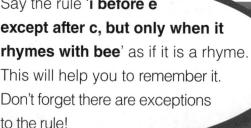

Top tip! Say the rule '**i before e except after c, but only when it rhymes with bee**' as if it is a rhyme. This will help you to remember it. Don't forget there are exceptions to the rule!

Listen up **29**

Keywords

Stress ➤ When you either increase the vowel length or loudness of the syllable, or both

Emphasis ➤ Stress

Syllable ➤ A single, unbroken sound containing a vowel (or y)

Words ending in fer

When you add a suffix to a word ending in **fer**, it is helpful to say the word aloud to identify where the **stress** or **emphasis** falls so you can decide whether you need to double the **r**. If the **syllable fer** is still <u>stressed</u> after the suffix is added, the **r** is doubled.

refer ⟶ refer**r**al (stressed so double r)

prefer ⟶ <u>pref</u>erence (not stressed so single r)

transfer ⟶ trans<u>fer</u>**r**ed (stressed so double r)

infer ⟶ <u>inf</u>erence (not stressed so single r)

The manager signed the player who had trans**fer**red from another team, despite his pre**fer**ence to stay put.

Top tip!

Seeing the relationship between words in the same word families can help you with spelling, e.g. medicine – medical – medication.

Have a go!

Create a table with the headings:

ei after soft c	i before e	ei ay sound	ei ee sound

Find as many words for each column as you can.

Test yourself

① Circle the correct spelling of the underlined words in these sentences.

a. The passenger <u>preffered / preferred</u> <u>transferring / transfering</u> her suitcase using the <u>unwieldy / unweildy</u> trolley.

b. I kept <u>receiving / recieving</u> letters with a <u>wierd / weird</u> stamp advertising <u>abseiling / absieling</u> events.

Letter string ough

The letter string **ough** is one of the trickiest to spell, especially as it can be used to spell a few different sounds.

fought	rough	cough	thorough	plough	through
bought	enough	trough	borough	bough	dough

Say this sentence out loud to hear the different sounds from the **ough** letter string. Can you find the sounds **oh**, **aw**, **uff**, **ow** and **off**?

Alth**ough** Oliver th**ough**t the sea was r**ough**, he was a t**ough** sailor who pl**ough**ed on, despite his bad c**ough**.

Silent letters

Some letters that were sounded hundreds of years ago are no longer sounded today. These **silent letters**, however, often remain in the words. The word **knight**, for example, used to be pronounced with a hard **k** sound whereas now we say it exactly like we would say **night**. The spellings of such words might not make a lot of sense but they just have to be learned! The study of the origin of words, and the way in which their meanings and sounds have changed throughout history, is called **etymology**.

Look at these words containing silent letters:

knot   **g**narl   **g**nome   com**b**

We**d**nesday   han**d**kerchief

Letter string psych

The letter string **psych** comes from Greek and is always a tricky one to spell! You just have to learn it.

psychology   **psych**iatrist   **psych**ic   **psych**edelic

The letters ph

We know that **ph** is pronounced as an **f** sound, even though it seems strange; these words stem from Ancient Greek.

phonics   **ph**iloso**ph**y   apostro**ph**e   geogra**ph**y

There is one exception to the pronunciation of **ph** – the name **Stephen** is pronounced with a **v** sound.

Keyword

Silent letter ➤ A letter that was once pronounced but now isn't

Top tip!

It can help you spell words containing silent letters if you pronounce them in your head when you are learning them.
Say **cup-board** and **Wed-nes-day**, pronouncing the **p** and **d**.

Have a go!

Choose a page from your reading book or a newspaper and see how many silent letters you can find.

Test yourself

❶ The underlined words in these sentences have been spelled as they sound. Use the <u>ough</u> letter string to correct them.

a. He <u>bawt</u> lots of water, just in case, because he <u>thawt</u> there would be a <u>drowt</u>.

b. Phillip <u>brawt</u> lots of <u>coff</u> sweets but there weren't <u>enuf</u> to go around.

c. Andrew searched the <u>troff</u> <u>thurully</u> but couldn't see the treasure he <u>sawt</u>.

d. We <u>fawt</u> long and hard against the <u>tuff</u>, <u>ruf</u> soldiers, <u>plowing</u> on until we'd captured them all.

Words ending in o

- As a general rule, most nouns ending in **o** add **s** in the plural. Many of these words originate from other languages.

  avocado —————————→ avocado**s**

  zero —————————→ zero**s**

  My mum bought some avocados from the market.

- Even those with a vowel before the **o** just add **s**.

  studio —————————→ studio**s**

  zoo —————————→ zoo**s**

- However, some nouns ending in **o** gain the letters **es** in the plural.

  potato —————————→ potato**es**

  tomato —————————→ tomato**es**

- Others are acceptable with either an **s** or **es**.

  mango —————————→ mango**s** / mango**es**

  volcano —————————→ volcano**s** / volcano**es**

  Last year Dad grew his own tomatoes.

Latin words – plural endings

Some Latin nouns that we use in English form their plural in the Latin way, by adding an **e**.

alga —————————→ alga**e**

larva —————————→ larva**e**

antenna —————————→ antenna**e**

Ants use their antennae to navigate.

Words ending in f

- When a word ends in **f**, we usually change the **f** to **v** and add **es** or **s** to make it plural.

  loaf ⟶ loa**ves**

  thief ⟶ thie**ves**

  wife ⟶ wi**ves**

  wolf ⟶ wol**ves**

- There are exceptions:

  chief ⟶ chief**s**

  roof ⟶ roof**s**

- Some words can have either ending:

  scarf – scarf**s** / scar**ves**

  dwarf – dwarf**s** / dwar**ves**

  hoof – hoof**s** / hoo**ves**

  We heard the wolves howling all through the night.

Learn the **exceptions** to the **f** ⟶ **v** rule, then it's easy to remember to apply it!

Listen up
31

Have a go!

What is the rule for changing single nouns ending in <u>o</u> to the plural?

Test yourself

① Write the plurals of the following words.

  a. knife

  b. armadillo

  c. leaf

  d. calf

Homophones

Homophones are words that sound the same but have different spellings and different meanings.

> hair and hare

If you do not spell these words correctly, it could be confusing for the reader.

> Standing **here** I could not **hear** the **whales' wails**.

Here are some common homophones.

two	to	too	
pour	pore	paw	poor
groan	grown		
reins	reigns	rains	
cereal	serial		
there	their	they're	
altar	alter		
isle	aisle		
ascent	assent		
weather	whether		
draft	draught		
aloud	allowed		
rowed	road		

Tricky homophones

Some homophones are super tricky because, even though they don't sound exactly the same, they sound similar enough that people often misspell them. They are called **near homophones**.

- affect – usually a verb
- effect – usually a noun

The weather can **affect** some people's mood. A sunny day can have such a positive **effect**.

Parent tip!

Do bear in mind regional accents when discussing whether two words sound similar or the same.

Keywords

Homophones ➤ Words that sound the same but have different spellings and different meanings

Near homophones ➤ Words that sound almost the same as another

practice – noun

practise – verb

licence – noun

license – verb

Top tip!

To help you remember practi**c**e / practi**s**e:
- practi**c**e with a **c** is a **n**oun; **c** comes before **n** in the alphabet
- practi**s**e with an **s** is a **v**erb; **s** comes before **v** in the alphabet.

Listen up
32

Have a go!

Explain what a near homophone is.

Test yourself

❶ **Choose the correct word from these near homophones.**

a. I <u>guessed / guest</u> that we wouldn't have maths today.

b. It had <u>passed / past</u> half <u>past / passed</u> nine but we didn't take the <u>advice / advise</u> of our teacher.

c. The new Head Teacher had an amazing <u>affect / effect</u> on the children.

Vocabulary and Spelling

This mind map will help you remember all the main points from this topic. Have a go at drawing your own mind map.

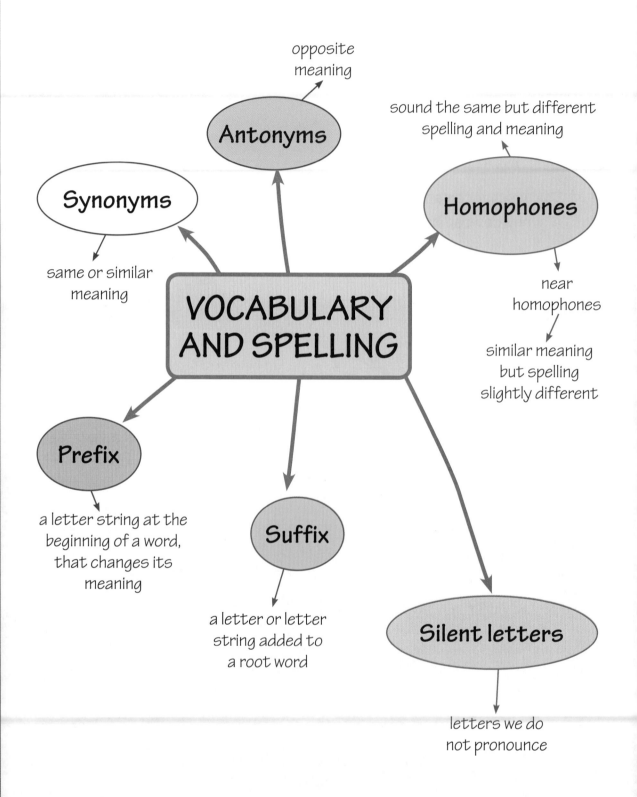

opposite meaning

Antonyms

sound the same but different spelling and meaning

Homophones

Synonyms

same or similar meaning

VOCABULARY AND SPELLING

near homophones

similar meaning but spelling slightly different

Prefix

a letter string at the beginning of a word, that changes its meaning

Suffix

a letter or letter string added to a root word

Silent letters

letters we do not pronounce

1 Use an appropriate prefix to change the meaning of these words. **(4 marks)**

happy	....
understand	....
appropriate	....
polite	....

2 Write a synonym for each of these words. **(4 marks)**

breezy ....

angry ....

supple ....

considerate ....

3 Underline the two incorrect words in these sentences then write the correct homophones.

a. We eight our pairs and went to bed. **(1 mark)**

....

....

b. They're hare has been cut very short. **(1 mark)**

....

....

4 Write an antonym for each of the following words. **(4 marks)**

high	....
smooth	....
rigid	....
frenzied	....

5 Spell the underlined words correctly. **(2 marks)**

We have only **brawt** our **ruff** sketches, **althow** if we have **enuff** time we **awt** to be able to complete them.

....

....

6 Insert the correct homophones in the sentence below. **(1 mark)**

draft / draught   **through / threw**

A .... blew .... the open window.

1 Replace the underlined word or words in the sentences below by writing the correct **pronoun** in each box. **(1 mark)**

....

Grace took off her coat then <u>Grace</u> sat down by the fire. Her mum

brought her a sandwich and she ate <u>the sandwich</u> hungrily.

....

2 Tick the sentence that uses the correct **plural**. **(1 mark)**

Have you seen those peoples swimming? ☐

I saw six gooses crossing the river. ☐

The farm dog rounded up all the sheep. ☐

We saw the thiefs leaving the bank. ☐

3 Complete the passage with **adjectives** derived from the nouns in brackets. One has been done for you. **(1 mark)**

Stanley and I were very ___**cautious**___ [caution] as we climbed down

the cliff. Wilf, however, was so .... [enthusiasm] that

he nearly fell over! As we clambered closer to the bottom, we were

.... [excitement] to see the crashing waves.

4 Underline two **adverbs** in this sentence. **(1 mark)**

Eventually, the children stopped shivering and cautiously crossed the stream.

5 Circle the word in the passage that contains an **apostrophe** for **possession**. **(1 mark)**

Let's go to the park. We'll play on the swings and the slide until

it's time to go home. Sofia's mum will pick us up.

6 Draw a line to match each sentence to the correct **determiner**. Use each determiner only **once**. **(1 mark)**

Sentence

The children stood before .... ancient castle.	
Mum came for .... walk with me.	
Here is .... book that you lent me.	

Determiner

the
an
a

7 Complete the sentences below using the **simple past tense** of the verbs in the boxes. **(1 mark)**

kick	throw	catch

Sami .... the ball over the hedge. Our neighbour

.... it back to him and he .... it.

8 Rewrite the sentence below so that it is in the **active voice**. Remember to punctuate your sentence correctly. **(1 mark)**

Luke was given an award by the Head Teacher.

....

9 Find the **subject** and the **object** in this sentence then write them in the table below. **(1 mark)**

Joseph quickly finished his homework.

Subject	
Object	

10 Which sentence uses the **comma** correctly? Tick **one**.　**(1 mark)**

I'm off, to buy some bread although I suspect the shop will be closed. ☐

I'm off to buy some bread, although I suspect the shop will be closed. ☐

I'm off to buy some bread although I suspect, the shop will be closed. ☐

I'm off to buy, some bread, although I suspect the shop will be closed. ☐

11 Insert **inverted commas** in the correct places in this sentence.　**(1 mark)**

I wish Joe would hurry up, thought Brogan impatiently.

12 Underline the **subordinate clause** in the sentence below.　**(1 mark)**

As we were driving to school, we noticed that someone had

fallen on the footpath.

13 Which sentence is punctuated correctly? Tick **one**.　**(1 mark)**

As he walked towards the Church, tom was aware that he was being followed. ☐

As he walked towards the church, Tom was aware that he was being followed. ☐

As he walked towards the church Tom was aware that he was being followed. ☐

As he walked, towards the church, tom was aware that, he was being followed. ☐

14 a. What is the **name** of the punctuation marks on either side of the words *who is only eight* in the sentence below? **(1 mark)**

My little brother (who is only eight) can dive from the top diving board.

....

b. What is the name of a different punctuation mark that could be used correctly in the same places? **(1 mark)**

....

15 Insert two **commas** to clarify this sentence. **(1 mark)**

The teacher having no reason to think otherwise believed the children were telling the truth.

16 Replace the underlined words in the sentence below with their **expanded forms**. **(1 mark)**

We've got to be at the cinema by 9pm or we'll miss the start of the film.

....

....

17 Which sentence uses the **present perfect form**? Tick **one**. **(1 mark)**

We went shopping for some new clothes. ☐

Mum has been learning to speak Italian. ☐

I have made a new friend at school. ☐

Martha is often late in the morning. ☐

18 Complete the table by writing suitable **synonyms**. **(1 mark)**

Word	Synonym
sturdy	
unsure	

19 Circle the two **conjunctions** in the sentence below. **(1 mark)**

Stella likes oranges and apples but not pears.

20 What type of words are **up** and **on** in the following sentence?
Tick the correct answer. **(1 mark)**

I flew up the stairs and collapsed on my bed.

prepositions ☐

conjunctions ☐

pronouns ☐

synonyms ☐

21 Which sentence is grammatically correct? Tick **one**. **(1 mark)**

Stella's bike is more impressive than Erin's. ☐

Stella's bike is impressiver than Erin's. ☐

Stella's bike is most impressive than Erin's. ☐

Stella's bike is most impressiver than Erin's. ☐

22 Insert a **semi-colon** in the correct place in the sentence below.   **(1 mark)**

I just love going to the countryside it truly is a delight each time.

23 Tick one box in each row to show whether the sentence is written in the **active voice** or the **passive voice**.   **(1 mark)**

Sentence	Active	Passive
I ran in a cross-country race at the weekend.		
First prize was won by my friend, Dan.		
I won second prize.		

24 Which sentence shows that you are **most likely** to go to Scotland on holiday this year? Tick **one**.   **(1 mark)**

I might go to Scotland for my holiday this year.   ☐

I could go to Scotland for my holiday this year.   ☐

I may go to Scotland for my holiday this year.   ☐

I shall go to Scotland for my holiday this year.   ☐

GRAMMAR TERMS

Test Yourself Questions

page 5

1 Accept appropriate nouns, e.g. ball (common noun), William (proper noun), honesty (common noun that cannot be seen or touched)

2 **a.** astronauts (common noun); Mars (proper noun); photographs (common noun); Earth (proper noun)

 b. Ben (proper noun); courage (common noun); bees (common noun)

page 7

1 **a.** I was drinking my juice when the phone rang.

 b. Suddenly, the car crashed into the brick wall.

 c. I eat my tea every evening before I watch television.

 d. While we were having a picnic it started to rain.

 e. Joe was jumping on his trampoline when it began to rain.

page 9

1 **a.** I am <u>definitely</u> unable to go swimming tonight.

 b. He'll <u>likely</u> come tomorrow.

 c. <u>Perhaps</u> if you tried harder you would succeed.

 d. You should <u>probably</u> leave early tomorrow because it is going to snow.

page 11

1 Once the <u>electric</u> fence had been activated, even the most <u>desperate</u> animals couldn't escape.

2 Accept two appropriate sentences using interesting adjectives.

3 Answers will vary. Examples:

 a. My cat is much naughtier than your dog./ My cat is the naughtiest cat in the world.

 b. My cat is more sensible than yours./My cat is the most sensible cat in the world.

page 13

1 A main clause makes sense on its own. A subordinate clause cannot stand alone.

2 Answers will vary. Examples: and, but, or, because, although.

3 Answers will vary. Examples: I like bread **but** I don't like toast. You won't be allowed to play out **unless** you do your homework.

page 15

1 it – the gloomy distance; them – Fred and Aisha

2 That bike isn't yours! That bike is mine!

3 The boys' books, **which** were scattered all over the floor, had been expensive birthday presents.

page 17

1 **a.** <u>Desperately</u>, Erin wriggled <u>through the gap</u> and <u>in a matter of minutes</u> was free.

 b. <u>In the middle of the night</u>, the wind <u>suddenly</u> died down and <u>soon</u> the children were fast asleep.

2 Answers will vary. Example: Dev decided he wanted to go **somewhere** warm and sunny.

3 Answers will vary. Example: When he got to the Caribbean, Dev found it **extremely** hot.

page 19

1 I went <u>to</u> my room and <u>in</u> it was the biggest mess imaginable! After I had cleared it, I went <u>to</u> the kitchen and sat <u>at</u> the table. Later, Mum called me to help <u>in</u> the garden. What a day!

page 21

1 <u>Some</u> children were heading towards <u>the</u> beach when <u>an</u> adult came towards them waving <u>a</u> flag. It was <u>the</u> coastguard. He told them <u>the</u> weather had changed and they couldn't go in <u>the</u> sea. <u>The</u> children turned back up <u>the</u> path.

2 The determiner **an** is used before a noun beginning with a vowel when we are not referring to a specific object.

Practice Questions

page 23

1

Proper nouns	Common nouns	
	Nouns we can see or touch	Nouns we can't see or touch
Antarctica	flock	strength
Prince George	hand	despair
July	flower	fear
Jupiter	dog	bravery
United Kingdom	house	pity

(3 marks: award 2 marks for 10–11 correctly placed nouns and 1 mark for 7–9)

2 I ate my dinner quickly. **(1 mark)**

3 a. My mother <u>could</u>n't finish the horror story.

   b. The heating has been on so you <u>must</u> be warm now.

   c. <u>Would</u> it be possible to leave the theatre now?

(3 marks)

4 Answers will vary. The sentence should include a main clause which makes sense on its own and a subordinate clause introduced by a conjunction such as because, although, even though… and so on.

Example:
We decided to walk the dog, even though it was getting close to bedtime. **(1 mark)**

5 We had salad <u>and</u> bread for tea <u>but</u> nothing at bedtime. The next morning we were tired <u>and</u> hungry. There was some cereal on the table <u>yet</u> no sign of any milk. **(2 marks for all 4 conjunctions; 1 mark for up to 3)**

6 My sister hurt her finger at the park and <u>she</u> had to have <u>it</u> bandaged. The nurse praised <u>her</u> for being brave and <u>she</u> gave <u>her</u> a special plaster.

(2 marks for all 5 pronouns correctly underlined; award only 1 mark for at least 3 pronouns)

7 Harry tiptoed <u>carefully</u> down the creaky steps. He <u>soon</u> reached the cellar where he stumbled <u>awkwardly</u> over a <u>carelessly</u> discarded pizza box.

(2 marks: award only 1 mark for 2 correctly identified)

CREATING SENTENCES

Test Yourself Questions

page 25

1 a. where the boy was – <u>beside her</u> / <u>on the bus</u>.

   b. what Christa was worried about – <u>the bad-tempered boy</u>.

2 Subordinate clause

page 27

1 a. My neighbour, **who** is old and unsteady, needs help in his garden.

   b. The kite, **which** was brightly coloured, danced on the breeze.

   c. My dog, **who** is called Benji, is very giddy.

page 29

1 Accept appropriate questions. Examples:

   a. What do horses eat?

   b. Where is Australia?

   c. What time do you go to bed?

Practice Questions

page 31

1 Accept appropriate adjectives to form expanded noun phrases. Examples:

   a. the fluffy rabbit

   b. a thrilling funfair

   c. some chatty teachers

   d. a fluttering butterfly

(4 marks)

2 Sam scrambled <u>with great caution</u> over the rocks.

(1 mark)

3

Sentence	Main clause	Subordinate clause
Although it was almost home time, **the teacher began a new chapter of the book**.	✓	
As they were expecting friends, **James and Jules tidied their rooms**.	✓	
Stella forgot to hand in her library book **because she was in a hurry to get home**.		✓

(3 marks)

4 a. The homework, **which** we all found difficult, is due in first thing in the morning.

   b. My Aunty Vivienne, **who** came to tea yesterday, has been taken to hospital.

   c. The school caretaker, **whose** shed was destroyed by vandals, still has a smile on her face.

(3 marks)

5

Sentence	Statement	Question	Command	Exclamation
Erin, finish brushing your teeth now!			✓	
How much longer until we arrive?		✓		
I have just bought a new bike.	✓			
How silly my little brother is at times!				✓

(4 marks)

6 Answers may vary. Examples:

   a. My aunty is coming for tea later **because/as** it's my mum's birthday.

   b. You can't go out **as/because/if/while** it is raining so heavily.

   c. We can't get into school **until/unless** the caretaker opens the door.

   d. We were told to stand at the back of the classroom **even though/although** it wasn't actually us who had been talking.

(4 marks)

SENTENCE FEATURES

Test Yourself Questions

page 33

1 a. <u>The children</u> **are** dancing to the music.

   b. <u>You</u> **have** been very well-behaved today.

   c. Running down the road **was** <u>a herd of cows</u>.

   d. <u>I</u> **do** my homework every night.

page 35

1 a. <u>My dog</u> (subject) gnawed his (bone) (object).

   b. <u>We</u> (subject) all told (him) (object) not to run!

   c. <u>Flooding</u> (subject) is damaging many (homes) (object).

   d. <u>The weather announcer</u> (subject) presented a (temperature graph) (object).

page 37

1 a. Passive
   b. Active
   c. Active
   d. Passive

page 39

1 a. "There will be no school due to the heavy snow," the Head Teacher told his staff.

   b. "Get your homework done immediately or there will be no TV," said my mum.

   c. "You have parked on double yellow lines," grumbled the traffic warden.

   d. "You are ready to take your diving badge," my swimming instructor told me.

page 41

1 Accept appropriate sentences in Standard English. Examples:

   a. The Head should let us have a snow day!

   b. It is at least one metre deep and my mother's car is broken.

   c. Alright, we will see what happens but I am definitely not going in!

Practice Questions

page 43

1 a. You **go** to the cinema every Saturday.

   b. We **were** hoping to finish early today.

   c. I **saw** a massive spider.

(3 marks)

2 a. The children persuaded the puppy to stop eating the toy.

   b. Our teachers asked us to submit two more pieces of work.

   c. The firemen had lifted the children to safety so they were out of danger.

(3 marks)

3

Subjects	Objects
Ciara	cliff
She	waves
a bird	hair

(3 marks)

4 Accept appropriate informal speech. Example:

We have to leave at 7.00 pm on the dot. If anyone's late, there'll be trouble. We've got to make sure that nobody spills the beans.

(2 marks)

5 a. "You played brilliantly in defence, Sarah!" said the referee. **(1 mark)**

   b. "The holiday you like the best is out of our price range," explained our parents.

(1 mark)

PUNCTUATION

Test Yourself Questions

page 45

1 Inverted commas can be used as additional punctuation as long as positioned accurately.
   a. What was the score?
   b. What an amazing match that was!
   c. I can't wait to phone Uncle Eric! Do you think he'll be home from work?

page 47

1 Douglas and Emily, who were brother and sister, were going camping for the weekend. Between them they packed: sleeping bags, jumpers, walking boots, a Thermos flask, snacks and a camera.

page 49

1 Accept inverted commas in correct positions, such as at end of speech, but after final comma or other punctuation mark.
   "There really isn't much point in packing a picnic," said Joe.
   "Well, it's not going to rain forever," replied Dylan.
   "Look over there – I can see a patch of blue sky!"
   "Good for you," Joe said grumpily. "Do you really think that means the sun will come out?"

page 51

1 Jake's mum's chicken pie wasn't the best. She'd burnt its edges as she'd left it in the oven too long. They should've gone out to Charlie's Chippy, thought Jake.

page 53

1 Accept appropriate choice of parentheses and subordinate clauses in context; **b.** has to be brackets.
   a. I couldn't be bothered to go swimming – I was feeling a bit under the weather – so I stayed at home.
   b. We were amazed by the trapeze artists at the circus (they were a big improvement on last year's).
   c. Having been there on holiday before, a couple of times in fact, we knew our way around.

page 55

1 Accept appropriate choice of punctuation such as:
   a. My father and I play football at the weekend; he is the goalkeeper and I am the striker.
   b. We turned the corner and there it was – a wild-eyed creature, foaming at the mouth.
   c. The ingredients are: flour, eggs, milk and sugar.

page 57

1 well-known, sport-mad, brother-in-law, bad-tempered

Practice Questions

page 59

1 The term 'apostrophes for possession' means using an apostrophe to show ownership. **(1 mark)**

2 a. "We're going to eat, Dad," said the hungry children. **(1 mark)**
   b. The girls were looking forward to chicken, potatoes, peas and some cold juice. **(1 mark)**
   c. The rescue boat, a vessel the coastguards had been using for many years, swiftly reached the canoe. **(1 mark)**
   d. This school, according to its website, expects a high standard of behaviour. **(1 mark)**

3 We've been looking at holidays – we are thinking of Spain, France or Italy. **(1 mark)**

4 We are really leaning towards a trip to Spain; we were there last summer. **(1 mark)**

5 Other options for our holiday are the following: Croatia, Portugal and Bulgaria. **(1 mark)**

6 The rule for hyphenating words at the end of a line is hyphenate after a syllable and never hyphenate before a single letter. **(1 mark)**

7 Accept an appropriate sentence showing a colon used correctly. Example: to introduce a list. **(1 mark)**

VOCABULARY AND SPELLING

Test Yourself Questions

page 61

1 Accept any appropriate antonym. Examples:

Word	Antonym
sad	happy
extrovert	introvert
exciting	dull
stormy	calm

page 63

1 a. sister liberi – irresistible
   b. little aire – illiterate
   c. rail ration – irrational
   d. glaci olli – illogical

page 65

1 a. reliable, reliably
   b. desirable, desirably
2 a. audible, audibly
   b. visible, visibly

page 67

1 a. residential
   b. facial
   c. sacrificial
   d. influential
2 a. adherence
   b. reliance

page 69

1 a. The passenger (preferred) (transferring) her suitcase using the (unwieldy) trolley.

  b. I kept (receiving) letters with a (weird) stamp advertising (abseiling) events.

page 71

1 a. He **bought** lots of water, just in case, because he **thought** there would be a **drought**.

  b. Phillip **brought** lots of **cough** sweets but there weren't **enough** to go around.

  c. Andrew searched the **trough thoroughly** but couldn't see the treasure he **sought**.

  d. We **fought** long and hard against the **tough**, **rough** soldiers, **ploughing** on until we'd captured them all.

page 73

1 a. knives

  b. armadillos

  c. leaves

  d. calves

page 75

1 a. I **guessed** that we wouldn't have maths today.

  b. It had **passed** half **past** nine but we didn't take the **advice** of our teacher.

  c. The new Head Teacher had an amazing **effect** on the children.

Practice Questions

page 77

1

happy	**unhappy**
understand	**misunderstand**
appropriate	**inappropriate**
polite	**impolite**

(4 marks)

2 Suggested answers:
breezy – windy
angry – cross
supple – flexible
considerate – kind / thoughtful   **(4 marks)**

3 a. We <u>eight</u> our <u>pairs</u> and went to bed.
          ate   pears

  b. <u>They're hare</u> has been cut very short.
       Their   hair   **(2 marks)**

4 Suggested answers:

high	**low**
smooth	**rough**
rigid	**soft / bendy**
frenzied	**calm**

(4 marks)

5 We have only **brought** our **rough** sketches, **although** if we have **enough** time we **ought** to be able to complete them.   **(2 marks)**

6 A **draught** blew **through** the open window.
     (1 mark)

SATs PRACTICE QUESTIONS

pages 78–83

1 Grace took off her coat then <u>she</u> sat down by the fire. Her mum brought her a sandwich and she ate <u>it</u> hungrily.   **(1 mark)**
(Do not accept capitalisation of inserted pronouns 'she' or 'it', or incorrect spelling of the pronouns.)

2 The farm dog rounded up all the sheep. ☑
     (1 mark)

3 Stanley and I were very <u>cautious</u> as we climbed down the cliff. Wilf, however, was so <u>enthusiastic</u> that he nearly fell over! As we clambered closer to the bottom, we were <u>excited</u> to see the crashing waves. **(1 mark)**

4 <u>Eventually</u>, the children stopped shivering and <u>cautiously</u> crossed the stream.
     (1 mark)

5 Let's go to the park. We'll play on the swings and the slide until it's time to go home. (Sofia's) mum will pick us up.   **(1 mark)**

6
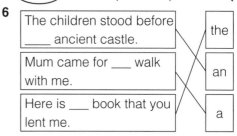

(1 mark)

7 Sami **kicked** the ball over the hedge. Our neighbour **threw** it back to him and he **caught** it.   **(1 mark)**

8 The Head Teacher gave Luke an award.
     (1 mark)

(The sentence must be correctly punctuated for the mark to be awarded.)

9

Subject	Joseph
Object	his homework

(1 mark)

10 I'm off to buy some bread, although I suspect the shop will be closed. ☑ **(1 mark)**

11 "I wish Joe would hurry up," thought Brogan impatiently.   **(1 mark)**

12 <u>As we were driving to school</u>, we noticed that someone had fallen on the footpath.
     (1 mark)

13 As he walked towards the church, Tom was aware
that he was being followed. ☑ **(1 mark)**

14 a. brackets **(1 mark)**

  b. Accept either: (a pair of) commas; (a pair of)
  dashes **(1 mark)**

15 The teacher, having no reason to think otherwise,
believed the children were telling the truth. **(1 mark)**

16 We have got to be at the cinema by 9pm or **we will**
miss the start of the film. **(1 mark)**

17 I have made a new friend at school. ☑ **(1 mark)**

18 Suggested answers:

Word	Synonym
sturdy	strong
unsure	uncertain

(1 mark)

19 Stella likes oranges (and) apples (but) not pears.

(1 mark)

20 prepositions ☑ **(1 mark)**

21 Stella's bike is more impressive than Erin's. ☑

(1 mark)

22 I just love going to the countryside; it truly is a delight
each time. **(1 mark)**

23

Sentence	Active	Passive
I ran in a cross-country race at the weekend.	✓	
First prize was won by my friend, Dan.		✓
I won second prize.	✓	

(1 mark)

24 I shall go to Scotland for my holiday this year. ☑

(1 mark)

Glossary

Abbreviations – Shortened word forms

Active voice – Where the subject of the sentence is doing or being something

Adjective – A word that describes a noun

Adverb – A word that tells us more about a verb (how, where, when), an adjective, another adverb or a whole clause

Adverbial – A word, phrase or clause that gives us more information about a verb (how, where, when, how often) or clause

Ambiguity – Having more than one meaning

Antonym – A word that means the opposite to another word

Apostrophe – A punctuation mark used to show omission (contraction) or possession

Brackets – Punctuation mark used to show parenthesis

Bullet points – Used to draw attention to items in a list

Capital letters – Letters in upper case, used at the start of sentences and proper nouns

Clause – Contains a verb and can be a main clause or subordinate clause

Colloquialisms – Expressions in informal, everyday language

Colon – Introduces a clause that gives detail or introduces a list, a quotation or speech in a play script

Comma – Punctuation mark used to separate items in a list; in direct speech; to show a brief pause; to separate a main clause from a subordinate clause and to indicate parenthesis

Command – A sentence that gives an instruction

Common nouns – Nouns for people, animals and objects

Conjunction – Links two words, phrases or clauses

Contraction – A word that has been made shorter

Coordinating conjunction – Links two words, phrases or clauses of equal importance

Dash – Punctuation mark used to show a break or pause in a sentence

Determiner – A word that introduces a noun such as 'the', 'a', 'some' and 'those'

Dialogue – A conversation between two or more people

Direct speech – A sentence in inverted commas showing the exact words spoken by someone

Ellipsis – The omission of text, sometimes shown by three dots (...)

Emphasis – Stress

Exclamation – A sentence that shows feelings like fear, anger, happiness or excitement

Exclamation mark – Punctuation at the end of an exclamation or command

Expanded noun phrase – A phrase with a noun as its main word with other words that tell us more about that noun

Formal speech – Speaking and writing using correct grammar and vocabulary

Fronted adverbial – An adverb or adverbial at the start of a sentence

Full stop – Punctuation at the end of a sentence

Homophones – Words that sound the same but have a different spelling and different meanings

Hyphen – A punctuation mark that links words to make some compound words, to join prefixes to some words or to show a word break at the end of a line

Hyphenated compound words – Two words combined with a hyphen to make one new word

Informal speech and writing – A relaxed, chatty way of speaking and writing used with family and friends

Inverted commas – Used on either side of a sentence or phrase to show that someone is speaking

Main clause – A clause that can make sense as a sentence

Modal verbs – Verbs that show possibility or likelihood

Near homophones – A word that sounds almost the same as another

Noun phrase – A phrase where a noun is the main word

Nouns – Naming words for people, places, animals and things

Object – A noun, pronoun or noun phrase showing what the subject is acting upon

Omission – Leaving letters or words out

Parentheses – The punctuation marks used to indicate parenthesis

Parenthesis – A word or phrase inserted into a sentence as an explanation or afterthought

Passive voice – When the subject isn't carrying out the action but is being acted upon by someone or something

Past – A verb tense showing what has happened

Past perfect – A verb tense formed from the past tense of the verb 'have' + the past participle of the main verb

Past progressive – A verb tense showing a continuous action in the past

Phrase – A group of words that work together as if they are one word

Possession – Ownership

Possessive determiner – Shows ownership of the noun that immediately follows

Possessive pronoun – A word to show ownership

Prefix – A string of letters added to the start of a word to change its meaning

Preposition – Shows the relationship between the noun or pronoun and other words in the clause or sentence

Present – A verb tense showing what is happening now

Present perfect – A verb tense formed from the present tense of the verb 'have' + the past participle of the main verb

Present progressive – A verb tense showing a continuous action in the present

Pronoun – A word that replaces a noun

Proper nouns – Nouns that name particular things. They begin with a capital letter

Punctuation marks – 'Signposts' to help us understand text

Question – A sentence that asks something

Question mark – Punctuation mark at the end of a question

Relative clause – A subordinate clause introduced by a relative pronoun

Relative pronoun – The words 'who', 'which', 'that' and 'whose', which introduce a relative clause

Root word – A word in its own right, without a prefix or a suffix

Semi-colon – Links two closely related sentences or separates items in a list where some items might be longer than one or two words

Silent letter – A letter that was once pronounced but now isn't

Slang – Very informal language used when speaking to friends

Speech marks – Used on either side of a sentence or phrase to show that someone is speaking

Standard English – Using the rules of English correctly

Statement – A sentence that gives information

Stress – When you either increase the vowel length or loudness of the syllable or both

Subject – The person or thing that is doing or being something in the sentence

Subjunctive – A verb form that shows a wish or an imaginary state

Subordinate clause – A clause which depends on the main clause to make sense

Subordinating conjunction – Joins a subordinate clause to a main clause

Suffix – A letter or a string of letters added to the root word to change or add to its meaning

Syllable – A single, unbroken sound containing a vowel (or y)

Synonym – A word that means the same or almost the same as another word

Thesaurus – A book of words and their synonyms

Verb – A word for an action or state of being